THE HISTORY & CULTURE
of NATIVE AMERICANS

The
Zuni

THE HISTORY & CULTURE of NATIVE AMERICANS

THE HISTORY & CULTURE of NATIVE AMERICANS

The
Zuni

NANCY BONVILLAIN

Series Editor
PAUL C. ROSIER

CHELSEA HOUSE
An Infobase Learning Company

The Zuni

Chelsea House
An imprint of Infobase Learning
132 West 31st Street
New York, NY 10001

Library of Congress Cataloging-in-Publication Data

Bonvillain, Nancy.
  The Zuni / Nancy Bonvillain.
    p. cm.—(The history and culture of Native Americans)
  Includes bibliographical references and index.
  ISBN 978-1-60413-799-6 (hardcover)
  1. Zuni Indians—Juvenile literature. I. Title. II. Series.

  E99.Z9B665 2011
  978.9004'97994—dc22

                         2010044826

Chelsea House books are available at special discounts when purchased in bulk quantities for businesses, associations, institutions, or sales promotions. Please call our Special Sales Department in New York at (212) 967-8800 or (800) 322-8755.

You can find Chelsea House on the World Wide Web at http://www.infobaselearning.com

Text design by Lina Farinella
Cover design by Alicia Post
Composition by Newgen
Cover printed by Yurchak Printing, Landsville, Pa.
Book printed and bound by Yurchak Printing, Landsville, Pa.
Date printed: May 2011
Printed in the United States of America

10 9 8 7 6 5 4 3 2 1
This book is printed on acid-free paper.

All links and Web addresses were checked and verified to be correct at the time of publication. Because of the dynamic nature of the Web, some addresses and links may have changed since publication and may no longer be valid.

Contents

Foreword

by Paul C. Rosier

Native American words, phrases, and tribal names are embedded in the very geography of the United States—in the names of creeks, rivers, lakes, cities, and states, including Alabama, Connecticut, Iowa, Kansas, Illinois, Missouri, Oklahoma, and many others. Yet Native Americans remain the most misunderstood ethnic group in the United States. This is a result of limited coverage of Native American history in middle schools, high schools, and colleges; poor coverage of contemporary Native American issues in the news media; and stereotypes created by Hollywood movies, sporting events, and TV shows.

Two newspaper articles about American Indians caught my eye in recent months. Paired together, they provide us with a good introduction to the experiences of American Indians today: first, how they are stereotyped and turned into commodities; and second, how they see themselves being a part of the United States and of the wider world. (Note: I use the terms *Native Americans* and *American Indians* interchangeably; both terms are considered appropriate.)

In the first article, "Humorous Souvenirs to Some, Offensive Stereotypes to Others," written by Carol Berry in *Indian Country Today,* I read that tourist shops in Colorado were selling "souvenir" T-shirts portraying American Indians as drunks. "My Indian name is Runs with Beer," read one T-shirt offered in Denver. According to the article, the T-shirts are "the kind of stereotype-reinforcing products also seen in nearby Boulder, Estes Park, and likely other Colorado communities, whether as part of the tourism trade or as everyday merchandise." No other ethnic group in the United States is stereotyped in such a public fashion. In addition, Native people are used to sell a range of consumer goods, including the Jeep Cherokee, Red Man chewing tobacco, Land O'Lakes butter, and other items that either objectify or insult them, such as cigar store Indians. As importantly, non-Indians learn about American Indian history and culture through sports teams such as the Atlanta Braves, Cleveland Indians, Florida State Seminoles, or Washington Redskins, whose name many American Indians consider a racist insult; dictionaries define *redskin* as a "disparaging" or "offensive" term for American Indians. When fans in Atlanta do their "tomahawk chant" at Braves baseball games, they perform two inappropriate and related acts: One, they perpetuate a stereotype of American Indians as violent; and two, they tell a historical narrative that covers up the violent ways that Georgians treated the Cherokee during the Removal period of the 1830s.

The second article, written by Melissa Pinion-Whitt of the *San Bernardino Sun,* addressed an important but unknown dimension of Native American societies that runs counter to the irresponsible and violent image created by products and sporting events. The article, "San Manuels Donate $1.7 M for Aid to Haiti," described a Native American community that had sent aid to Haiti after it was devastated in January 2010 by an earthquake that killed more than 200,000 people, injured hundreds of thousands more, and destroyed the Haitian capital. The San Manuel Band of Mission Indians in California donated $1.7 million to help relief efforts in Haiti; San Manuel children held fund-raisers to collect additional donations. For the San Manuel Indians it was nothing new; in 2007 they had donated $1 million to help Sudanese refugees in Darfur. San Manuel also contributed $700,000 to relief efforts following Hurricane Katrina and Hurricane Rita, and donated $1 million in 2007 for wildfire recovery in Southern California.

Such generosity is consistent with many American Indian nations' cultural practices, such as the "give-away," in which wealthy tribal members give to the needy, and the "potlatch," a winter gift-giving ceremony and feast tradition shared by tribes in the

Pacific Northwest. And it is consistent with historical accounts of American Indians' generosity. For example, in 1847 Cherokee and Choctaw, who had recently survived their forced march on a "Trail of Tears" from their homelands in the American South to present-day Oklahoma, sent aid to Irish families after reading of the potato famine, which created a similar forced migration of Irish. A Cherokee newspaper editorial, quoted in Christine Kinealy's *The Great Irish Famine: Impact, Ideology, and Rebellion,* explained that the Cherokee "will be richly repaid by the consciousness of having done a good act, by the moral effect it will produce abroad." During and after World War II, nine Pueblo communities in New Mexico offered to donate food to the hungry in Europe, after Pueblo army veterans told stories of suffering they had witnessed while serving in the U.S. armed forces overseas. Considering themselves a part of the wider world, Native people have reached beyond their borders, despite their own material poverty, to help create a peaceful world community.

American Indian nations have demonstrated such generosity within the United States, especially in recent years. After the terrorist attacks of September 11, 2001, the Lakota Sioux in South Dakota offered police officers and emergency medical personnel to New York City to help with relief efforts; Indian nations across the country sent millions of dollars to help the victims of the attacks. As an editorial in the *Native American Times* newspaper explained on September 12, 2001, "American Indians love this country like no other. . . . Today, we are all New Yorkers."

Indeed, Native Americans have sacrificed their lives in defending the United States from its enemies in order to maintain their right to be both American and Indian. As the volumes in this series tell us, Native Americans patriotically served as soldiers (including as "code talkers") during World War I and World War II, as well as during the Korean War, the Vietnam War, and, after 9/11, the wars in Afghanistan and Iraq. Native soldiers, men and women, do so today by the tens of thousands because they believe in America, an

America that celebrates different cultures and peoples. Sgt. Leonard Gouge, a Muscogee Creek, explained it best in an article in *Cherokee News Path* in discussing his post-9/11 army service. He said he was willing to serve his country abroad because "by supporting the American way of life, I am preserving the Indian way of life."

This new Chelsea House series has two main goals. The first is to document the rich diversity of American Indian societies and the ways their cultural practices and traditions have evolved over time. The second goal is to provide the reader with coverage of the complex relationships that have developed between non-Indians and Indians over the past several hundred years. This history helps to explain why American Indians consider themselves both American and Indian and why they see preserving this identity as a strength of the American way of life, as evidence to the rest of the world that America is a champion of cultural diversity and religious freedom. By exploring Native Americans' cultural diversity and their contributions to the making of the United States, these volumes confront the stereotypes that paint all American Indians as the same and portray them as violent; as "drunks," as those Colorado T-shirts do; or as rich casino owners, as many news accounts do.

*   *   *

Each of the 14 volumes in this series is written by a scholar who shares my conviction that young adult readers are both fascinated by Native American history and culture and have not been provided with sufficient material to properly understand the diverse nature of this complex history and culture. The authors themselves represent a varied group that includes university teachers and professional writers, men and women, and Native and non-Native. To tell these fascinating stories, this talented group of scholars has examined an incredible variety of sources, both the primary sources that historical actors have created and the secondary sources that historians and anthropologists have written to make sense of the past.

Although the 14 Indian nations (also called tribes and communities) selected for this series have different histories and cultures, they all share certain common experiences. In particular, they had to face an American empire that spread westward in the eighteenth and nineteenth centuries, causing great trauma and change for all Native people in the process. Because each volume documents American Indians' experiences dealing with powerful non-Indian institutions and ideas, I outline below the major periods and features of federal Indian policy making in order to provide a frame of reference for complex processes of change with which American Indians had to contend. These periods—Assimilation, Indian New Deal, Termination, Red Power, and Self-determination—and specific acts of legislation that define them—in particular the General Allotment Act, the Indian Reorganization Act, and the Indian Self-determination and Education Assistance Act—will appear in all the volumes, especially in the latter chapters.

In 1851, the commissioner of the federal Bureau of Indian Affairs (BIA) outlined a three-part program for subduing American Indians militarily and assimilating them into the United States: concentration, domestication, and incorporation. In the first phase, the federal government waged war with the American Indian nations of the American West in order to "concentrate" them on reservations, away from expanding settlements of white Americans and immigrants. Some American Indian nations experienced terrible violence in resisting federal troops and state militia; others submitted peacefully and accepted life on a reservation. During this phase, roughly from the 1850s to the 1880s, the U.S. government signed hundreds of treaties with defeated American Indian nations. These treaties "reserved" to these American Indian nations specific territory as well as the use of natural resources. And they provided funding for the next phase of "domestication."

During the domestication phase, roughly the 1870s to the early 1900s, federal officials sought to remake American Indians in the mold of white Americans. Through the Civilization Program, which actually started with President Thomas Jefferson, federal officials sent religious missionaries, farm instructors, and teachers to the newly created reservations in an effort to "kill the Indian to save the man," to use a phrase of that time. The ultimate goal was to extinguish American Indian cultural traditions and turn American Indians into Christian yeoman farmers. The most important piece of legislation in this period was the General Allotment Act (or Dawes Act), which mandated that American Indian nations sell much of their territory to white farmers and use the proceeds to farm on what was left of their homelands. The program was a failure, for the most part, because white farmers got much of the best arable land in the process. Another important part of the domestication agenda was the federal boarding school program, which required all American Indian children to attend schools to further their rejection of Indian ways and the adoption of non-Indian ways. The goal of federal reformers, in sum, was to incorporate (or assimilate) American Indians into American society as individual citizens and not as groups with special traditions and religious practices.

During the 1930s, some federal officials came to believe that American Indians deserved the right to practice their own religion and sustain their identity as Indians, arguing that such diversity made America stronger. During the Indian New Deal period of the 1930s, BIA commissioner John Collier devised the Indian Reorganization Act (IRA), which passed in 1934, to give American Indian nations more power, not less. Not all American Indians supported the IRA, but most did. They were eager to improve their reservations, which suffered from tremendous poverty that resulted in large measure from federal policies such as the General Allotment Act.

Some federal officials opposed the IRA, however, and pushed for the assimilation of American Indians in a movement called Termination. The two main goals of Termination advocates, during the 1950s and 1960s, were to end (terminate) the federal reservation system and American Indians' political sovereignty derived from treaties and to relocate American Indians from rural reservations to urban areas. These coercive federal assimilation policies in turn generated resistance from Native Americans, including young activists who helped to create the so-called Red Power era of the 1960s and 1970s, which coincided with the African-American civil rights movement. This resistance led to the federal government's rejection of Termination policies in 1970. And in 1975, the U.S. Congress passed the Indian Self-determination and Education Assistance Act, which made it the government's policy to support American Indians' right to determine the future of their communities. Congress then passed legislation to help American Indian nations to improve reservation life; these acts strengthened American Indians' religious freedom, political sovereignty, and economic opportunity.

All American Indians, especially those in the western United States, were affected in some way by the various federal policies described above. But it is important to highlight the fact that each American Indian community responded in different ways to these pressures for change, both the detribalization policies of assimilation and the retribalization policies of self-determination. There is no one group of "Indians." American Indians were and still are a very diverse group. Some embraced the assimilation programs of the federal government and rejected the old traditions; others refused to adopt non-Indian customs or did so selectively, on their own terms. Most American Indians, as I noted above, maintain a dual identity of American and Indian.

Today, there are more than 550 American Indian (and Alaska Natives) nations recognized by the federal government. They have a legal and political status similar to states, but they have special rights and privileges that are the result of congressional acts and the hundreds of treaties that still govern federal-Indian relations today. In July 2008, the total population of American Indians (and Alaska Natives) was 4.9 million, representing about 1.6 percent of the U.S. population. The state with the highest number of American Indians is California, followed by Oklahoma, home to the Cherokee (the largest American Indian nation in terms of population), and then Arizona, home to the Navajo (the second-largest American Indian nation). All told, roughly half of the American Indian population lives in urban areas; the other half lives on reservations and in other rural parts of the country. Like all their fellow American citizens, American Indians pay federal taxes, obey federal laws, and vote in federal, state, and local elections; they also participate in the democratic processes of their American Indian nations, electing judges, politicians, and other civic officials.

This series on the history and culture of Native Americans celebrates their diversity and differences as well as the ways they have strengthened the broader community of America. Ronnie Lupe, the chair of the White Mountain Apache government in Arizona, once addressed questions from non-Indians as to "why Indians serve the United States with such distinction and honor?" Lupe, a Korean War veteran, answered those questions during the Gulf War of 1991–1992, in which Native American soldiers served to protect the independence of the Kuwaiti people. He explained in "Chairman's Corner" in the *Fort Apache Scout* that "our loyalty to the United States goes beyond our need to defend our home and reservation lands. . . . Only a few in this country really understand that the indigenous people are a national treasure. Our values have the potential of creating the social, environmental, and spiritual healing that could make this country truly great."

—Paul C. Rosier
Associate Professor of History
Villanova University

Zuni Creation

In the beginning, say the Zuni, the only being who lived was *Awonawilona,* a deity both male and female. Nothing else existed, except some fog and steam. Then Awonawilona created the clouds and waters from its breath, and the rest of the universe was formed.

The universe created by Awonawilona consists of nine layers. The earth, a large circular island surrounded by oceans, occupies the middle level. The lakes, rivers, and springs on the earth connect underground to the oceans. The sky layer is an upside-down bowl of stone, resting above the earth. The other layers of the universe are each home to different kinds of animals, birds, and trees.

At first, people lived under the earth's surface in the fourth and innermost layer of the universe, deep inside the body of Earth Mother. The people did not look like humans today. Instead, their bodies were covered with slime, and they had tails and webbed hands and feet. They had no idea how strange they looked because it was dark where they lived and they could not see well. Then the Sun Father decided to bring the people out to the surface of the earth because he was lonely and had no one to give him offerings and prayers. Sun Father told his twin sons, the War Gods, to lead the Zuni out from inside the earth. The War Gods helped the people climb up a ladder to the surface and, once they were there, changed their appearance. The slime on the people's bodies disappeared, and their hands and feet became normal. Deities and priests instructed the people to recite prayers, make offerings, and conduct ceremonies to honor Sun Father and other spirit powers. In return, the spirits gave people blessings and protection.

The Zuni remained near their place of emergence for a time. Then the deities told the Zuni to go forth and find the middle place, or *itiwana,* of the world, where they should build their villages. Important holy men called Rain Priests led the people on a journey that took many years. Each time they chose a place to settle, some misfortune occurred that forced them to move again. These misfortunes were signs from the spirits that the people had not yet found the itiwana of the world.

At last, the Zuni met an old man who was a powerful Rain Priest. When the Zuni's own Rain Priest prayed with the old man, a heavy rainstorm fell. Suddenly, a water spider came by, spread out its six legs, and told the people that the itiwana was directly under its heart. The Zuni knew its message to be true and set about building their villages. They built one village at the itiwana and six others at locations marked off by the legs of the water spider.

The Zuni then erected an altar at the exact site of the itiwana. On the altar, they placed sacred objects belonging to the Rain Priests as reminders of the people's journey and of their duty to honor the powerful deities who led them there. The altar remains today at the center of the village of Zuni. On it rests a stone that contains the eternal beating heart of the itiwana of the world.

The Zuni's story of their creation, emergence, and discovery of the itiwana situates them literally in the center of the world. Not surprisingly, they feel a strong spiritual and emotional connection

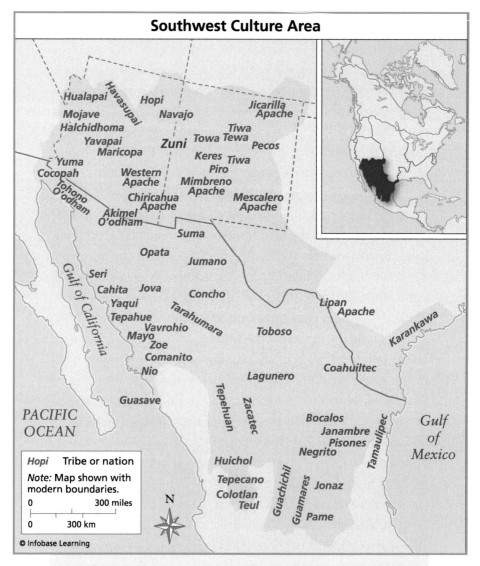

Southwest Culture Area

Hualapai
Havasupai
Hopi
Jicarilla Apache
Mojave
Navajo
Halchidhoma
Tiwa
Yavapai
Zuni
Towa Tewa
Pecos
Maricopa
Keres Tiwa
Yuma
Piro
Cocopah
Western
Mimbreno
Apache
Tohono O'odham
Apache
Chiricahua
Apache
Mescalero Apache
Akimel O'odham
Suma
Opata
Jumano
Seri
Cahita Jova
Concho
Yaqui
Tarahumara
Lipan Apache
Tepahue
Karankawa
Vavrohio
Toboso
Mayo
Zoe
Comanito
Nio
Coahuiltec
Lagunero
Guasave
Tepehuan
Zacatec
PACIFIC
OCEAN
Bocalos
Janambre
Gulf
of
Mexico
Pisones
Negrito
Tamaulipec

Hopi Tribe or nation
Huichol
Note: Map shown with modern boundaries.
Tepecano
Guachichil
Guamares
Jonaz
0   300 miles
Colotlan
N
0   300 km
Teul
Pame

© Infobase Learning

Early members of the Zuni lived in nomadic groups around the Zuni River in western New Mexico. Later, after developing farming techniques to supplement local food sources, they established themselves in permanent villages.

to their locale. They and their ancestors lived for centuries on lands along the banks of the Zuni River in western New Mexico. Their beautiful homeland contains a diversity of terrain and resources, including flat plains, plateaus, deserts, woodlands, foothills, and mountains. On the plains and desert grasslands grow shrubs, herbs, cactus, rabbitbrush, and yucca. Oak, spruce, juniper, and piñon trees are abundant in the woodlands and mountainous regions. Many animals inhabit the mountains and foothills, including elk, deer, antelope, mountain sheep, bears, and foxes. Rabbits, mice, squirrels, and reptiles abound in all areas.

Today, the Zuni reside in one large town, called Zuni, and several smaller villages located along nearby rivers and streams. Before the arrival of Europeans in the early sixteenth century, the Zuni lived in six villages, all within a 25-mile (40-kilometer) area and with access to good farmland. Zuni territory extended well beyond the villages, to the Zuni Mountains in the east and north, and the lower, more desertlike area to the west and south.

THE DESERT TRADITION

The Zuni made good use of the resources available in their territory. Their earliest ancestors arrived in the Southwest approximately 10,000 years ago. These early inhabitants created a civilization known to archaeologists as the Desert Tradition. Desert Tradition sites have been discovered at Concho in present-day eastern Arizona and at Bat Cave and Tularosa Cave in northern and central New Mexico. During the Desert period, people did not have permanent settlements. They moved their camps from time to time, adjusting their settlements to changes in plant growth and animal populations. Because of the scarcity of permanent sources of food, the camps were small, consisting of no more than a few families. The Desert peoples hunted animals—including several species of now-extinct horses, elephants, and great bison—for meat and for hides to use as clothing and shelter. They also gathered wild plants to eat and invented specialized technologies for preparing and cooking plant foods. One such technology that has survived to modern times is the *metate,* a specialized grinding stone used to make meal from different seeds and nuts.

Thousands of years after Desert Tradition peoples first entered the American Southwest, their descendants learned how to grow some of their own food. The earliest evidence of farming in the region dates from approximately 5,000 years ago. The people apparently borrowed farming methods from other tribes living farther south in present-day Mexico. These techniques gradually spread into the Southwest through a process called cultural diffusion, or the borrowing of skills by one group of people from neighboring groups.

The first plant grown by Native American farmers was corn—in fact, for about 2,000 years corn was the only crop cultivated in North America. Then, about 3,000 years ago, Native American farmers began to cultivate varieties of beans and squash. These three plants—corn, beans, and squash—have remained staples of southwestern cuisine, including that of the modern Zuni. Although Desert peoples farmed, they combined farming with their earlier way of life, continuing to hunt animals, gather wild plants, and live in small nomadic groups. Then, around 300 B.C., for reasons that remain unknown, a profound cultural change took place in the societies of the American Southwest. A new culture called the Mogollon Tradition developed. Mogollon peoples, who were ancestors of the modern Zuni, added many innovations to the Desert Tradition, changing their settlements, economies, and technology.

THE MOGOLLON TRADITION

The most obvious contrast between the Mogollon and Desert cultures is that Mogollon peoples lived in permanent villages. They built small settlements of approximately 100 people, living in rectangular or circular houses made of clay and stone. Ruins of Mogollon villages have been found at Forestdale and Black River in Arizona and at Cibola and Mimbres in New Mexico.

Farming and agricultural products became more central to the lives and economies of the Mogollon peoples. Corn was prepared by first drying and crushing the kernels and then grinding them into meal using a grinding stone. The resulting cornmeal was moistened with water and cooked on heated stones. Fresh corn was also simply roasted over coals. Mogollon peoples dried beans to preserve them for later use; when they wanted to prepare the dried beans for meals, they soaked and boiled them in water. Squash was either boiled in water when fresh or dried for later use. Squash seeds, which are higher in calories, vitamins, and calcium than the flesh, were dried and stored for winter meals. Besides the staples of corn, beans, and squash, Mogollon peoples grew tobacco as well as cotton and sunflowers, which were cultivated for their vitamin- and calorie-rich seeds.

The Mogollon peoples expanded their inventory of tools and utensils. They made dishes, hammers, axes, hoes, bows, arrows, and a variety of grinding utensils, such as metates, mortars, and pestles from stone, wood, bone, and shell. Mogollon artists used tools to carve masks and effigies from stone and wood, and weavers used cotton (also introduced to the area by Mexican Indians) to make both plain and fancy cloth. Besides these innovations, the Mogollon peoples began to make earthen pottery, forming pots, bowls, and jars of different sizes and shapes to use for cooking and for carrying and storing food and supplies.

By A.D. 700 or 800, the Zuni's Mogollon ancestors had established permanent settlements in present-day Zuni territory. One such settlement is a village called White Mound, which contains groups of pit houses made of sandstone blocks and slabs and dug several feet into the ground to protect residents against outside cold and heat. In each house, a series of rooms 10 to 12 feet (3 to 3.7 meters) across is arranged in a line. A single nuclear family probably lived in each room, and a house probably held a group of related families. In addition to the pit houses, storerooms were built at ground level to hold equipment and dried foods. Farmland was located outside the clusters of houses and storerooms.

Other Mogollon villages in present-day Zuni territory include Kiatuthlanna, built in A.D. 800 or 900. Kiatuthlanna was larger than

The lives of the Zuni improved after they learned how to make pottery to hold water and food. Traditional Zuni pottery is considered an art form and is now a major source of income for many Zuni.

White Mound; an estimated 75 to 100 people lived in its 18 homes. In a later village named Allantown, built around A.D. 1000, houses constructed at ground level had begun to replace pit houses as the typical form of residence. Allantown and other Mogollon villages also contained *kivas,* special buildings where religious ceremonies were held.

Many innovative pottery designs, especially painted motifs, have been unearthed in Mogollon village digs. The artists initially used white paste and mineral paints to make black-on-white designs, but they eventually developed the use of green- and cinnamon-colored glazes. The designs themselves also changed, from thin lines to wider and blockier configurations that included geometric shapes and naturalistic figures.

ANASAZI TRADITION

Another new culture developed in the American Southwest around 1100. Called the Anasazi Tradition, it covered a large area, including present-day New Mexico, most of Arizona, and the southern portions of Utah and Colorado. The largest Anasazi villages were concentrated in the region known today as the Four Corners, where the states of Arizona, New Mexico, Utah, and Colorado meet. Well-known ruins of Anasazi settlements include those of Canyon de Chelly and Kayenta in Arizona, Mesa Verde in Colorado, and Chaco Canyon in New Mexico. While the Zuni's ancestors were on the periphery of Anasazi territory, they had contact with and were influenced by a number of Anasazi settlements, especially the one at Chaco Canyon.

Early in the Anasazi period, around 1100 or 1200, a Zuni settlement called the Village of the Great Kivas was built. The village contained three large masonry structures, varying in size from 6 to 60 rooms, all built at ground level, as well as nine round ceremonial kivas, seven of which were about the size of a single house. The remaining two kivas were much larger, measuring 51 and 78 feet (15.5 and 24 meters) in diameter, and were built in front of the village. These great kivas have benches attached to their interior walls, presumably for seating during rituals, and also contain two vaults beneath the main floor.

The thirteenth century was a period of rapid population growth in Zuni territory. By around 1275, a number of large, planned villages were constructed: Heshot Ula, Betatakin, and Kiet Siel. People from smaller settlements cooperated in the construction of these larger villages and then abandoned their original homes to take up residence in these towns.

In addition, the Zuni's ancestors built several villages in valleys along the Zuni River and its tributaries. Some settlements

Chaco Canyon, New Mexico *(above)*, was one of the largest Anasazi settlements in the Southwest. The architecture and organization of Chaco Canyon influenced the Zuni to build larger villages with pueblo homes.

were situated near cliffs to give residents protection from wind and snowstorms. By the thirteenth century, the Zuni's ancestors began to construct villages on top of mesas, giving the inhabitants a clear view of all approaches to the village and making defense of the village easier. One such village is Atsinna, located on a mesa known as Inscription Rock. The entire village of Atsinna formed a rectangle, measuring 215 by 300 feet (65.5 by 91 meters); its approximately 1,000 rooms were joined together in housing clusters. Some houses had only ground-floor rooms, while others had a second and third floor as well. The houses at Atsinna all faced inward, opening onto a large inner plaza.

Sometime in the fourteenth century, the Anasazi people in the Four Corners region suddenly abandoned their large towns and settled in smaller villages. The reason is not certain, but most modern researchers suggest that a drastic climatic change, most probably a series of lengthy droughts, impelled the move. Some Anasazi people then established villages along the Rio Grande in New Mexico, using water from the large river to irrigate their farms. Other people, including the Zuni and the nearby Hopi, remained away from the Rio Grande in the dry desert lands of New Mexico and Arizona.

Although the Zuni did not move to the Rio Grande, many people during this period did move from towns in the eastern half of Zuni territory to towns farther west. The six Zuni villages discovered by the Spanish conquistadores in the sixteenth century—Halona ("red ant place" and the home of the itiwana), Hawikuh, Kiakima ("house of eagles"), Matsaki, Kwakina ("town of the entrance place"), and Kechipauan ("gypsum place")—were established as a result of this migration.

TRADE TIES

Local and regional trade was an important feature of life in the American Southwest. The Zuni traded directly with their neighbors and, through trade networks, with Native Americans living in other areas. As early as A.D. 600–900, the Zuni's ancestors had trade relations with peoples in Mexico, California, and the Great Plains. By 1250, Zuni villages, especially Hawikuh, had become centers for intertribal trade and were visited by peoples from throughout the Southwest and adjacent regions. The Zuni traded corn, salt taken from Zuni Salt Lake (approximately 60 miles, or 97 kilometers, south of Halona), turquoise from local mines, and buffalo hides obtained by Zuni hunters on expeditions into the Great Plains, as well as cotton cloth, jewelry, baskets, pottery, moccasins, and a distinctive blue paint. In return, the Zuni received pottery, copper, and parrot feathers from Mexico; buffalo hides from the Great Plains; and seashells and coral from California.

The Zuni maintained peaceful relations with most of their neighbors in the Southwest. Many of these peoples, including the

Hopi, Tewa, Tano, and Keres, were culturally similar to the Zuni; consequently, these tribes are often grouped together as the Pueblo Indians. Although Pueblo Indians share many cultural features, they are distinct peoples and speak different languages—indeed, the Pueblo languages come from several entirely separate linguistic families, and Zuni is different from all other languages spoken in the region. Linguists today are uncertain as to whether Zuni is a language isolate, with no known connections to any other language, or whether it belongs to a language family called Penutian, in which case it is a remote relative of languages spoken in parts of California. The language of the nearby Hopi belongs to a family called Uto-Aztecan, distantly related to the language spoken by Aztecs in Mexico. The Pueblo Indians who live along the Rio Grande speak languages belonging to two other language families, Tanoan and Keresan. One result of the different languages used among the Pueblo Indians is that the Zuni are not called by the name they call themselves, the *A:shiwi* (pronounced with a long *a*). *Zuni* comes from a word in a Keresan language used by the Acoma Pueblo to refer to the A:shiwi; the Spanish picked it up from the Acoma, and it has since come into general use.

By the time the Spanish arrived to misname them, the Zuni had long established a stable, peaceful, and prosperous way of life in the itiwana of the world. Not only had they managed to develop the material resources of their relatively harsh surroundings, but they had also created a complex society intimately linked with their natural environment.

As we shall see, the Zuni's cultural resources were sorely tested beginning in the sixteenth century when Spanish explorers first ventured into their territory. In subsequent centuries, the Zuni had to struggle to retain their territories and to protect their way of life. They did so primarily on the strength of their families, their social systems that held their community together, and their religious beliefs that helped them endure.

The Zuni and
the Raw People

For the people of the itiwana, religion was the center of life, giving meaning to all activities. Success in farming, childbirth, and many other aspects of life was considered to be due to the aid of the Raw People, the Zuni name for the many powerful deities and spirits in their religion. These spirits were called Raw People because they ate raw foods as well as the cooked foods given to them as offerings by humans, who were called the Cooked People or Daylight People. Besides making offerings, humans expressed respect and gratitude to the Raw People by saying prayers and performing rituals in their honor. In exchange, the Raw People protected humans and gave them long lives, healthy children, personal courage, bountiful crops, successful hunts, and good fortune.

The many kinds of Raw People were associated with various natural forces or entities. Some Raw People were believed to be the spirits of animals, birds, or objects such as the sun, earth, and celestial bodies. Three very powerful Raw People were Earth Mother, Sun Father, and Moonlight-Giving Mother. Earth Mother was the place of life's origin, while Sun Father and Moonlight-Giving Mother provided humans light and good fortune (they were also husband and wife). Sun Father was considered especially important because he was the source of daylight, which the Zuni considered tantamount to life; indeed, the word for *daylight* and the word for *life* are the same in the Zuni language. Because of Sun Father's special role, sunrise was considered the most sacred time of day.

Other Raw People were associated with directions or with specific locations, such as lakes and mountains. According to Zuni cosmology, the world is oriented to six sacred directions: north, east, south, west, above (the zenith), and below (the nadir). Besides these directions, there is the itiwana, or middle, that connects the various elements of the universe. Directions in space help to set the boundaries of the world and to orient individuals to their places in it. Each direction is associated with certain colors, animals, birds, and trees. For the Zuni, this system of linkages underscored the spiritual unity and interconnection of all life in the universe.

The various elements of the world were kept alive and in balance by the efforts of the Raw People. In return for their protection and benevolence, the Zuni gave the Raw People offerings like cornmeal (sometimes mixed with crushed turquoise, shell, or coral), tobacco smoke, and small portions of cooked food. They also offered the deities sacred ceremonial sticks, called prayer sticks, that the men would make by carving faces into a piece of wood from a willow tree and decorating it with paint and feathers. Although only men could make the sticks, both women and men offered them to spirits or ancestors. The offering of prayer sticks formed an important part of many ceremonies, especially those marking the summer and winter solstices (June 21 and December 21).

The Zuni honored their deities, known as the Raw People, with ritual and offerings. Prayer sticks *(above)* were decorated with feathers and carvings to represent these spirits and were used in religious ceremonies.

MILESTONE RITUALS

Besides honoring the Raw People, Zuni rituals marked various critical stages in people's lives, including birth, puberty, marriage, and death. When a baby was born, its female relatives performed a variety of important duties. The baby's maternal grandmother would assist her daughter in the birth, but once the baby was born, its paternal grandmother would come to the home and recite prayers asking the Raw People to protect the baby. She would then bathe the baby, rub ashes on its body, prepare a bed of warm sand for it to lie in, and remain with mother and child for eight days. At sunrise on the eighth day after birth, the paternal grandmother would wash the baby's head, place cornmeal in its hands, and take the baby out into the dawn air, facing east toward the rising sun. While other female relatives sprinkled cornmeal toward the east, the grandmother would offer a prayer of blessing:

Now this is the day.
Our child,
Into the daylight
You will go standing.
Now this day
Our sun father,
Having come out standing to his sacred place,
Our child,
It is your day.
The flesh of the white corn,
Prayer meal,
To our sun father
This prayer meal we offer.
May your road be fulfilled
Reaching to the road of your sun father.

This prayer reflected a number of Zuni beliefs. The Zuni thought of life as a road that every individual follows according to his or her destiny. Sun Father assigned a specific road to each newborn baby, and all people hoped to live until they reached the proper end of their roads. Accidents or evil beings could interfere, however, and cause a premature death. Consequently, a newborn's grandmother prayed that her grandchild would be protected and allowed to live out his or her appointed road. The paternal grandmother also chose the baby's name, but babies were not immediately named after birth. Instead, the family would wait until they were sure that the infant was healthy and likely to survive. Usually, the name given the baby was the same as that of a relative on either side of the family who had lived a long life.

When a young Zuni girl reached puberty, another important set of rituals would take place. The adolescent girl would go to the home of her paternal grandmother, where she would spend a full day grinding corn—an act significant on both a secular and a religious level. Grinding corn into meal was one of the primary duties of Zuni women, so in completing this ritual, the girl would perform the practical work expected of adult women. The Zuni also considered corn a sacred plant, a gift brought to them by six Raw People known as the Corn Maidens. Corn was believed to be the flesh of these powerful Raw People and to have great spiritual power; consequently, it was used in practically every religious ceremony—and only women could keep, prepare, and distribute this essential substance. The performance of the corn-grinding ceremony thus indicated that a girl was now old enough to take on the important religious responsibilities of adult Zuni women, as well as their secular duties.

After a young lady reached puberty, she was deemed ready to become a wife, although marriages did not usually take place immediately. After a man and a woman decided that they wanted to marry, the woman would consult with her mother to make sure that the union met with the family's approval. Then for several weeks, the couple would attempt a trial marriage. The man would come to the woman's home at night, stay with her, and leave before dawn. During this time, either the man or the woman could choose not to marry. If the woman decided against marriage, the matter ended immediately, but if the man changed his mind, he had to give the woman a gift before the bond was broken.

In most cases, the couple would continue their relationship and become officially married. The Zuni marriage ceremony was fairly simple and was celebrated by various exchanges of gifts. Female relatives of the couple would give each other presents of food, clothing, and jewelry. As part of this ceremonial exchange of gifts, the woman would grind a large supply of corn to present to her mother-in-law. The mother-in-law would accept the cornmeal and give the bride a set of festive clothing. The couple would then return to the bride's home. The next morning the husband would leave after sunrise and return in the early evening to share dinner with his new family. At this point, the couple would be considered husband and wife by the community.

The ceremony could be further streamlined if a man decided to propose marriage without prior consultation or discussion. In this case, the man would simply bring a number of gifts to the woman's house and place them in the center of the room. The woman's father would then ask him to explain his intentions. The man would state his desire for marriage, and the father would respond, "It is up to my daughter." At that point, the woman could accept or reject the proposal.

Death among the Zuni marked a time of sorrow and solemn ritual, in contrast to the informality of marriage rites. The deceased person's paternal aunt would come to the home and bathe the body in suds made from a yucca plant. She would then rub corn-meal on the body and dress it in new clothes, making a gash in each garment so that the spirits of the clothes could accompany the person's soul on its journey to the afterworld. Relatives would come to the deceased's home and express their grief through words and tears, and the deceased's brothers would dig a grave and carry the body out for burial. The body was placed in the grave so that the head faced east, the direction of the rising sun. A number of the deceased's possessions were placed in the grave for the soul's use in the afterworld, while the rest of the deceased's personal belongings were later burned or buried in a separate spot.

After the burial, the surviving spouse observed a four-day period of intense mourning. The spouse had to stay away from fire, bathe only in cold water, avoid meat and salt, remain quiet, and keep away from others as much as possible. Most Zuni couples resided with the wife's relatives; consequently, if a wife died, the surviving husband had to leave the house and return permanently to his mother's or sister's home—a practice reflected in a

Important events in a Zuni's life are observed with detailed rituals. Death and burial ceremonies, for instance, involve specific relatives who must prepare the body and position it toward the east in the grave.

Zuni saying, "Death takes two, not one." The saying also reflected the belief that during the four days of mourning, the deceased's soul might try to take a companion, such as a close family member, along on the journey to the afterworld. During this period, the soul stayed in the village and sometimes made itself known to the living by scratching on surfaces, opening and closing doors, or appearing in dreams.

At the end of the four days, the soul would leave the village of the living and travel west to the village where souls reside. This village was at the bottom of a sacred lake, two days' journey from the town of Zuni. If the death was premature, however, the soul could not reach its final destination immediately but had to wait at a spot called Spirit Place, located 1 mile (1.6 kilometers) west of Zuni, until the time it should have reached the end of the road given to it at birth by Sun Father. When its appointed end finally came, the waiting soul could join its companions in the village under the lake.

HONORING THE SPIRITS

The Zuni believed that the living and the dead were eternally linked. The living had to honor the spirits of deceased ancestors, family members, and even enemy soldiers with prayers, food, and rituals performed for their pleasure. In return, the spirits would protect the living from harm and, if properly honored, would transform themselves into rain clouds and bless the living with valuable rainfall.

The living and the dead were connected in yet another way, through the *kachina* impersonators. According to Zuni myth, as the people wandered before finding the itiwana, some children were killed beside a lake. The itiwana was found, but the parents of the children missed them terribly and were always sad. To cheer them up, the spirits of the children (who had formed the village of souls underneath the lake) came to visit, bringing blessings and rainfall. These were the first kachinas (*kokko* in Zuni). Although their visits brought the Zuni much joy, the kachinas took the soul of a living person with them every time they returned to the village of the dead. The Zuni finally discussed this problem with the kachinas, who decided that they would no longer visit the Zuni in person but would only visit as rainfall. So that they might still enjoy dancing for the living, they allowed the Zuni to dress in their costumes and masks and perform their dances.

While wearing the masks and clothing, a person was spiritually transformed and took on some of the sacredness of the kachinas. The masks and costumes used by kachina dancers were made and handled with a great deal of care and religious ceremony; they were considered both sacred and alive, as well as capable of harming or killing a disrespectful dancer. In addition, kachina dancers had to perform intricate and lengthy public dances to honor the kachinas properly; these dances required days of rehearsal and sometimes lasted for hours. Creative Zunis could develop new dances, provided that religious leaders considered them appropriate, but the older forms were always thought to be more powerful and more sacred.

KACHINA SOCIETIES

All Zuni men were members of one of six kachina societies, which performed dances four times every year—just before the winter solstice, later in winter, in summer, and at harvesttime. On these days, the dancers donned their masks and costumes and entered the village at dawn. Led by their kachina chief and watched by almost everyone in the village, the dancers performed in the public plazas. While kachina dances obviously had great religious significance, they were also loved because of their beauty. Indeed, one purpose of the kachina dances was to provide entertainment for the village, and audience members could request that a particularly good dance be repeated again and again.

Kachina societies also held ceremonies in kivas. Each of the six kivas in Zuni was associated with a specific kachina society. Zuni kivas were special square-shaped rooms that were entered and exited by a ladder that extended through an opening in the ceiling; inside were large open spaces where dances and rituals were performed, with benches built against the walls to provide seating. In addition, kivas contained smaller rooms where highly secret rituals were conducted.

Zuni boys were inducted into kachina societies by their ceremonial fathers, a kind of godfather chosen by the boy's parents. A ceremonial father would induct his godson into his own kachina society when the boy was about five or six years old. During this initiation ceremony, the boy was washed by the wife of his ceremonial father, then carried by the ceremonial father to his kiva. Several boys were inducted at once, and when they all arrived at the kiva, adult members of the kachina society would enter dressed as kachinas and whip the boys to purify them. Although the whipping was usually painless, the experience was nonetheless intimidating for the boys, because they usually did not know that the

The Zuni Universe

According to Zuni beliefs, the earth is surrounded by an ocean inhabited by four giant feathered serpents of the colors yellow, blue, red, and white. Along the shores of the ocean live Rain Priests of the six directions (north, west, south, east, the zenith, and the nadir) who become clouds, rainstorms, fog, and dew when they leave their usual habitats. The Rain Priests are assisted by six Bow Priests, who create thunder and lightning.

The Zuni believe that the world is divided into six directions, each one associated with various colors, animals, birds, and trees. This system of linkages underscores a basic principle of Zuni philosophy, namely that all life is interconnected and unified by a spiritual order. The associations of directions, colors, and animal forms provide the basic symbolism of this unity. The associations include:

Direction	Color	Prey Animal	Game Animal
North	Yellow	Mountain Lion	Mule Deer
West	Blue	Bear	Mountain Sheep
South	Red	Badger	Antelope
East	White	Wolf	Whitetail Deer
Zenith	All Colors	Eagle	Jackrabbit
Nadir	Black	Mole	Cottontail Rabbit

kachinas were human impersonators. When the whipping ended, the ceremonial fathers would take the purified children home.

When the purified boys reached about 10 or 12 years of age, the second stage of initiation into the kachina societies occurred.

Direction	Bird	Tree
North	Oriole	Pine
West	Blue Jay	Douglas Fir
South	Parrot	Aspen
East	Magpie	Cottonwood
Zenith	Purple Martin	
Nadir	Swallow	

Every Zuni household keeps a sacred bundle that contains spiritually powerful objects and substances representing eternal natural and spiritual forces and the bounty of the universe. These bundles include water, plant seeds, stone-carved images of animals, and ceremonial masks. They are reminders of the sacred relationship between the Zuni and the deities, or Raw People, who guard and protect the people. The Zuni show their respect for the spirits and give thanks to them by making offerings of tobacco smoke, small portions of cooked food, and cornmeal that may be mixed with crushed jewels. People also sacrifice wooden prayer sticks that are painted, carved with faces, and decorated with feathers. Since the sticks represent the person making the sacrifice, the supplicant is essentially sacrificing a surrogate of himself or herself.

Women make special sacrifices to Moonlight-Giving Mother while men give to Sun Father. Everyone makes sacrifices to the ancestors, a generalized class of spirits. Offerings are always given at the summer and winter solstices, marking the changes in seasons and the earth's cycles. People may make offerings at many other times as well, if they are moved to do so.

The boys were again taken by their ceremonial fathers to the kivas and were whipped (usually more severely than during the initial purification) by the kachinas. This time, when the whipping ended, the impersonators would remove their masks, revealing to the boys that they were indeed human beings. The two groups then reversed roles, with the boys putting on the masks and whipping the adults. In this way, the boys gained the knowledge necessary for them to carry on the kachina society rituals.

OTHER RELIGIOUS SOCIETIES

The kachina societies were only six of the many Zuni religious societies. Each year, 12 Zuni men were chosen to impersonate six deities known as the *Shalakos*. The Shalakos were powerful, birdlike beings who performed dances in new homes built especially for them every year in the late fall. They brought good fortune, abundant crops, and many children. Shalako impersonators wore especially distinctive masks and costumes that made them over 10 feet (3 meters) tall.

Another special group of masked gods was made up of 10 ritual clowns called the Mudheads or *Koyemshis*. Unlike the Shalakos, the Koyemshis appeared in numerous dances and public rituals throughout the year, and different people could imitate a particular Koyemshi at different events. According to Zuni myth, the Koyemshis were the result of a sexual liaison between a brother and a sister, which made them both idiotic and impotent. Koyemshi impersonators wore mud-colored masks with foolish-looking faces and a short kilt of black cloth. Instead of wearing underclothes, Koyemshi impersonators had their penises tied down with cotton cord to symbolize the Koyemshis' childishness and infertility. Each Koyemshi had a distinct personality; for example, one was a coward, one was afraid of shadows and dark things, and one mistakenly believed that he was invisible. Koyemshi impersonators engaged in comical, outrageous, and often obscene behavior—exposing themselves, shouting obscenities, and making fun of spectators, kachina dancers, and priests.

Kachina dancers, dressed to represent the spirits of children who died in a Zuni myth, perform during ceremonies four times a year. Their dances, costumes, and masks are considered sacred.

The Zuni revered the Koyemshis despite their foolish and unacceptable behavior (which also served as an example of how not to act). The Koyemshis were believed to be Raw People of great antiquity, predating even the kachinas, and were consequently considered to have great power to bring fortune and rain. Their great power also made them potentially dangerous. At a certain point in the year, the Zuni were expected to give gifts to the Koyemshi impersonators. To begrudge the Koyemshis anything at this time, even in thought, was considered an invitation to disaster.

Another type of ritual clown was the *Neweekwe*. While they often appeared at the same events as the Koyemshis, the Neweekwes were not impersonators of Raw People but were instead members of perhaps the most remarkable of the many Zuni medicine societies. All of these societies performed dances and rituals intended to cure illness, but the Neweekwes were the only such society to engage in ritual clowning. Like the Koyemshi impersonators, members of the Neweekwe Medicine Society often behaved in a wild or obscene manner, but unlike the Koyemshis, they were not expected to take on specific personas. Consequently, the Neweekwes often engaged in far more sophisticated forms of clowning than the childish Koyemshis, including sometimes-biting parodies of current events. Since the Neweekwe Medicine Society specialized in curing stomach ailments, Neweekwe clowns would demonstrate the strength of their stomachs by drinking undrinkable fluids, such as urine, and eating inedible things, such as ashes, pebbles, wood chips, and feces.

Although most Zuni medicine societies did not go to the extremes of the Neweekwes in demonstrating their effectiveness, members of some medicine societies did engage in especially dramatic displays of their skills. Healers belonging to the Snake Medicine Society and the Little Fire Society bathed in fire, swallowed fire, and danced on hot coals without getting burned. Members of the Sword People bathed in icy water in the wintertime and swallowed swords and sticks without getting cut. These spectacular public rituals not only displayed the powers of the various medicine societies but were also believed to bring good health to the community in general. Both men and women could learn to perform these rituals by volunteering to join a medicine society. Besides learning a society's signature dramatic exploit, the members learned about the healing properties of roots, plants, massages, and rituals. Although some medicine societies relied more on medical cures and others more on ritual ones, every society had its specialty and would treat patients whenever its services were needed. Afterward, a patient who had received successful medical treatment from a society was often compelled to join that society.

The Zuni, like all peoples in the world, had a complex theory of causes and treatments of diseases. Most ailments were believed to have a spiritual cause; consequently, it was believed necessary to diagnose the cause accurately and treat it through religious ritual rather than simply eliminate obvious symptoms. Although many reasons for illness existed, most ailments were believed to result from the actions of spirits or witches. Spirits could harm someone who had violated ritual rules or had not properly honored deities and ancestors. Witches—spiteful, jealous, and malicious humans with magical knowledge—would cause harm in retaliation for a slight or out of envy for another's good fortune.

Spirits and witches often caused illness by magically shooting a foreign object, such as a pebble, a piece of wood, or a feather, into their victims. The harmful object had to be found and extracted for the patient to recover. Certain healers were able to see into a patient's body, locate the hidden object, and draw it to the surface either with an eagle feather or by sucking on the body. These healers gained their knowledge from the spirit of the bear, the most powerful of animal patrons.

Witches could also cause illness by reciting harmful spells over objects that had belonged to the intended victim, such as nail clippings, bits of hair, or pieces of clothing. Such spells could cause the victim to sicken or die. In this situation, a healer would try to break the spell through prayers and rituals. If the healer or patient knew the witch's identity, the patient's family could try to convince or force the witch into confessing and removing the spell.

PRIESTHOODS

Yet another important group of religious societies consisted of priesthoods. The most powerful was the Rain Priesthood—not surprising, given the importance of rain to the Zuni's survival. The Rain Priests were all men of high moral character; they avoided spiritually polluting arguments and conflicts and derived their knowledge and powers from the Rain-Bringing Spirits, who were among the most honored of deities.

One primary duty of the Rain Priests was to go on retreats to pray and perform rituals that would bring rain to the Zuni. Some rituals involved sacred bundles, which contained holy objects of great power, such as corn, cornmeal, seeds, feathers, prayer sticks, and stone effigies of spirit animals. The Rain Priesthood was made up of small groups of priests who would conduct four- or eight-day retreats in succession throughout the year, so that the community would never be without their spiritual aid.

Another prestigious group was the Bow Priesthood, which was believed to have obtained its power from the twin War Gods, who led the Zuni out of the earth in ancient times. Membership in the Bow Priesthood was required for warriors who had killed an enemy in combat; by joining the priesthood, the warrior received protection against the spirit of his deceased enemy, who would otherwise seek revenge. The responsibilities of the Bow Priesthood were more secular and more martial than those of the Rain Priesthood. Bow Priests were responsible for carrying out warfare and keeping order in the villages; guarding the many trails that the Zuni used to conduct local, regional, and long-distance trade; and implementing the decisions made by the Zuni's ruling council of religious leaders, which consisted of the heads of various religious orders, including the Rain Priesthoods, kachina societies, and medicine societies. Bow Priests also conducted the trials of people accused of witchcraft and performed the execution of unrepentant witches.

The Zuni's religious beliefs and practices helped keep their community strong and united. Private and public ceremonies were a focus of people's activities all year long, and anyone who was not planning, rehearsing, or conducting religious rituals at any given time participated as an audience member. Zuni religious societies also reduced potential conflicts within the community by forming bonds among their members, who might otherwise only have ties through family relationships. Consequently, disagreements that might arise almost never posed a serious threat to the basic unity and stability of the Zuni community.

Community Life

The people of the itiwana made good use of their land. For thousands of years, they grew crops, gathered wild plants, and hunted animals. They established small communities, developing strategies that enabled them to thrive in the sometimes unproductive environment of the American Southwest.

The Zuni divided most work along gender lines. While they believed that men and women were suited for different tasks, they also believed that gender was more of an acquired state than an innate one. Consequently, men who so wished could live as women, wearing women's clothes, performing work traditionally assigned to women, and even taking other men as husbands. Such people were called *lhamana* by the Zuni and were considered a gender distinct from males or females. Family members would sometimes encourage young boys who showed an interest in women's work or in behaving like women to become lhamanas (women in the family were often especially encouraging; lhama-nas were considered hard workers and a tremendous help around the house), but the boy himself made the final decision when he reached puberty. After a boy decided to become a lhamana, his religious education would continue as though he were a man, but his vocational education would be entirely that of a woman. The lhamana tradition eventually died out in the twentieth century due to the rabid opposition of U.S. authorities to the practice.

MEN'S WORK

The work of Zuni men centered on the production of food, and they prepared the land, planted seeds, and harvested crops. Some of these tasks were carried out by individuals, while other work, such as the preparation of fields for planting and the harvesting of crops, was done collectively, usually by a group of relatives.

The primary difficulty for Zuni farmers was not labor but the water supply. The climate in the Southwest is generally dry, with rainfall averaging only 10 to 15 inches (25 to 38 centimeters) per year. The rain that does fall often comes in sudden and severe storms in the summer months, which can drown or wash away young plants. The only other natural sources of water in the region are the small Zuni River and a few springs. To make the best use of available water, Zuni farmers developed a system of floodwater irrigation, which involved building small dams and canals with mud walls to direct water from rainfall and overflowing streams to the crops. This method was quite successful, and the Zuni culti-vated as many as 10,000 acres (4,046 hectares) of corn, producing a large enough surplus in good years to keep a two-year supply on hand in case of losses from drought or insect damage.

Besides farming, Zuni men hunted in the surrounding plains, deserts, and mountains. Hunting was usually done in groups, sometimes as large as 100 or 200 people. Closer to the villages, small animals, like rabbits, mice, and other desert rodents, were found in abundance, while the more distant woodlands and mountains contained large animals, such as deer, antelope, elk, mountain sheep, and bear. Zuni men hunted rabbits with sticks thrown like boomerangs and hunted deer by driving them into either fenced enclosures or pits dug in the ground, where they could easily be killed.

Men also fished in the Zuni River and its tributaries and snared birds, using delicate traps of wood and twine designed specifically for each species. They trapped eagles, ducks, wild turkeys, hawks, owls, crows, and blue jays, using their flesh for food and their feathers for decorating clothing and ceremonial equipment. Zuni families also kept flocks of domesticated turkeys, which all household members tended. These turkeys were raised mainly for their feathers, but when other food was scarce, they were also eaten.

WOMEN'S WORK

Zuni women were responsible for preparing, cooking, and preserving foods. One of their most time-consuming tasks was grinding corn. Many breads and cakes were made of cornmeal, and it took hours of careful work to produce an adequate amount. Different recipes called for different consistencies of cornmeal, ranging from coarse to very fine, and nuts and seeds were ground for food as well. As a result, a Zuni woman owned several grinding stones with varying edges to produce the different types of meal. Once the meal was ground, women would make it into batter to be either fried over a fire or baked in an oven.

Women also grew crops but only in small gardens generally located along the banks of the Zuni River. These gardens, called waffle gardens because of their distinct appearance, were divided into small square or rectangular cells surrounded by low mud walls that helped to conserve water and protect the plants from wind. Women watered their gardens by hand, using ladles to distribute water that they carried from the Zuni River or from nearby wells. They brought water to the gardens in jars called *ollas,* which they carried on their heads.

Besides growing crops, women gathered many varieties of wild plants growing near their villages. Some plants were used for medicinal purposes, such as ointments for burns and eye

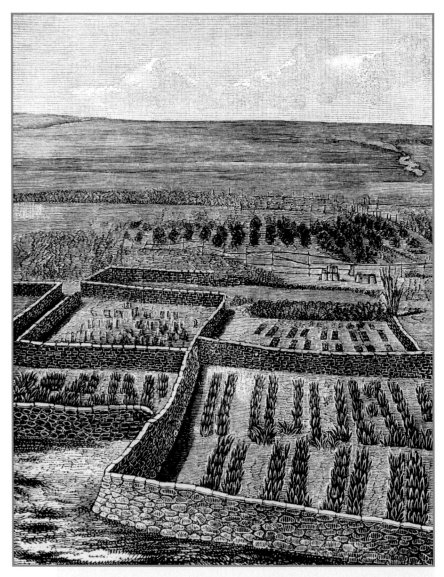

Zuni women tended to their own private gardens, known as waffle gardens. Because the Southwest received only a little rainfall each year, these gardens were often built next to the Zuni River.

irritations; painkillers for headaches, toothaches, and sore throats; salves to promote healing of wounds; and drugs to help women in childbirth. Other wild plants, such as nuts, watercress, yucca, juniper berries, sunflowers, wild rice, wild peas, wild potatoes, parsnips, and milkweed, were eaten as supplements to agricultural products and contributed valuable nutrients to people's diet. Because the Zuni relied on their corn and bean crops as their primary source of protein, nuts were especially important as an additional source of protein during crop failures.

Men and women each had specific duties when undertaking tasks such as building a house. The men built the outside structure of houses from sandstone blocks and slabs; then the women plastered the interior walls. The women were responsible for keeping up the plaster, applying fresh coats when the walls deteriorated over time. Women were also responsible for keeping a fire going to heat the houses in winter, but the men cut and hauled home the firewood.

Zuni women and men also specialized in different crafts. Women were the potters and were responsible for all stages of the pottery-making process, from the digging of clay to the final painting. Men made the tools and gear used for farming and hunting, including digging sticks, shovels, axes, bows, and arrows. Men also produced a variety of household utensils and personal items. They made baskets from twined and coiled yucca and rabbitbrush, and they wove the cotton cloth that was fashioned into blankets, clothing, and sashes. Finally, men used turquoise (obtained from the Zuni's mines and quarries, which also produced silver, copper, and obsidian), shell, and coral to craft beautiful jewelry that all Zuni wore. Both men and women wore cotton garments and deerskin- or antelope-hide footwear. Women wore cotton blouses, skirts, and sashes, while men wore cotton shirts, sashes, and aprons over deerskin leggings. Cloth was often dyed with bright mineral or vegetable pigments, and clothing was decorated with embroidered geometric designs.

A COMFORTABLE LIFE

By skillfully developing their crafts and making good use of their resources, the Zuni lived in prosperity. Their comfortable and

---

Zuni Corn

Although Zuni men planted a variety of crops, corn (*a'ta'a* or "the seed of seeds") was given the most attention, both in terms of human activity and ceremonial care. Farmers kept a store of seeds taken from all six varieties of corn (white, yellow, blue, red, black, and speckled), representing the most perfect ears grown in the previous harvest. The seeds were kept in a family "corn room" or "granary." They were prayed over when put away for storage and again when taken out for planting. As described in *Zuni: Selected Writings of Frank Hamilton Cushing* (the anthropologist who lived with the Zuni in the 1880s):

> The farmer next chose six kernels of corn, one of each of the different colors, proclaiming to the women there, "We go!" And, as he steps out of the doorway, the corn matron hustles after him with a bowl of fresh, cold water, with which she lavishly sprinkles him, laughingly telling them to go. Thoroughly bedrenched, he shuffles down the hill, across the river, and out to his field.

The seeds were sprinkled over in order to symbolize the rain needed to nourish and help them grow. The farmer planted the first seeds in small holes in the ground, covered the grains, and returned home, remaining away from the fields for four days, during which time he fasted and prayed at sunrise. When he finally returned to the fields, he buried the seeds in small holes dug 4 to 7 inches (10 to 18 centimeters) into the earth, putting some 15 to 20 kernels in each to ensure that at least some would yield plants.

secure way of life was described in 1540 by Francisco Vásquez de Coronado, a Spanish officer who led an expedition through the Southwest:

Groups of related men working together harvested the corn. They were usually either fathers and sons, brothers, cousins, or in-laws. The men husked some of the corn immediately in the fields so that the husks could decay and fertilize the earth, but most ears were taken back to the village, where groups of women husked and dried them. A large supply was kept in sealed storage rooms as a surplus to be used in years of poor harvests.

Corn was ground into cornmeal and made into a great variety of recipes. Traditional corn dishes, many still prepared today, are either cooked in large pots of boiling water, on flat stones in open fireplaces within homes, or inside dome-shaped ovens built outdoors on terraces. Boiled breads or dumplings are made from small balls of fine and coarse cornmeal and salt. After they are boiled in water, they harden and become somewhat pasty. Yellow cornmeal, sweetened with dried flowers, is made into a kind of pudding. The batter is then wrapped in green corn leaves and boiled or baked. Some types of corn bread are prepared with ashes or lime yeast used as a leavening.

After the flour is prepared, it is molded into thick cakes and cooked on hot coals or baked under hot ashes. The most prized corn bread is a delicacy called *hewe,* a paper-thin bread prepared on large baking stones. To make hewe, women grind all six varieties of corn into a fine flour that is then mixed with hot water to form a thin paste, which is finally poured onto heated cooking stones. As soon as the batter is lightly toasted, it is peeled away from the stone. Hewe is eaten on ceremonial and domestic occasions and is given as gifts in ritual exchanges.

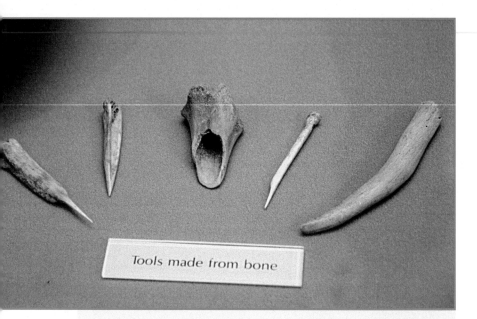

Tools made from bone

When fashioning household items or tools, the Zuni utilized whatever materials were available to them. Utensils could be made from bone, clay from the river was used for pottery, and sticks and stones could become axes and arrows.

They have very good homes and good rooms with corridors and some quite good rooms underground and paved, built for the winter. The town of Granada [Coronado's name for the Zuni village Hawikuh] has two hundred houses, all surrounded by a wall. There is another town nearby, but somewhat larger than this, and another of the same size as this; the other four are somewhat smaller.

The people of these towns seem to me to be fairly large and intelligent. They are well built and comely. I think that they have a quantity of turquoises.

The food which they eat consists of maize, of which they have great abundance, beans, and game. They make the best tortillas that I have ever seen anywhere. They have the very best arrangement and method for grinding that was ever seen. They have very good salt in crystals, which they bring from a lake a day's journey distant from here.

The "very good homes" Coronado saw reflected the Zuni's family structure in their architecture. A Zuni house usually had one, two, or three stories of rooms arranged in rows, and related families would occupy a series of adjacent rooms. Zuni families were considered related through the women—married daughters remained in the household into which they were born, but married sons usually left home and moved into their wives' households. A traditional Zuni household included an extended family made up of an elder couple, their daughters, their daughters' husbands and children, and their unmarried sons. Therefore, the eldest woman traditionally organized the activities of the residents and made sure that all necessary work was completed. She was also the person to consult for advice concerning problems or major decisions.

ZUNI KINSHIP

Besides the extended family, the Zuni's social system included kin groups called lineages. A lineage consists of people related by direct descent from a known ancestor or elder. Zuni lineages were matrilineal, or based on the principle of descent through women. The eldest surviving woman in a lineage was usually considered the head of that lineage and played an active role in the lives of its members by giving advice, settling disputes, and organizing group activities. In addition, the head woman would safeguard certain sacred objects that were considered the property of her lineage; these items were usually kept in a bundle placed on an altar erected in a special room of her house. The eldest brother of the head woman was also an important figure in a lineage and would also be consulted by lineage members faced with a conflict or an important decision.

These lineages were combined into larger kinship units called clans. A clan is a group of people who believe that they are related by descent from a common ancestor. A member of the more than a dozen Zuni clans could not always trace his or her specific familial relationship to every other member, but clan members believed they were all descendants of a specific figure of the ancient past. As with other Zuni kinship groups, Zuni clans were matrilineal, and

Zuni children automatically belonged to the clan of their mother. Nonetheless, the Zuni also had close ties to their father's group, and individuals often referred to themselves as a "child of my father's clan." Clan membership strongly affected people's choice of a marriage partner. Since members of a clan were considered relatives, they could not marry each other. In addition, the Zuni condemned marriages between a person and someone in his or her father's clan.

Besides their role in determining appropriate marriages, clans served several other functions in Zuni society. Each clan had control over certain areas of farmland within Zuni territory. The elder women of a clan, who were the clan heads, distributed the land to the lineages and households within their group. Plots of farmland were controlled and could be inherited by the women of an individual household, but these plots were not truly private property belonging to individuals. Rather, land was considered a resource ultimately controlled by the clan as a whole, and members of the clan had the right to use the land according to their needs. Although the women of a household inherited the farmland, the men did the farmwork. A man would work on his mother's land until he married, at which time he would move into his wife's household and work on her family's land.

Because Zuni relatives lived and worked together and shared food and other goods, family members tended to be deeply loyal and emotionally close to each other. Bonds between parents and sons and between sisters and brothers also remained strong even when a man left the household after marriage. Men were expected to return frequently to their first home to help celebrate family occasions and to give aid to their relatives. Indeed, if a man came from an important family that looked after especially sacred objects, he could easily spend more time with (and gain more status from) his own family than his wife's.

The importance of kinship in Zuni life was reflected in how people addressed each other. Words used to address close relatives were also used to address other people in the clan. For example, Zunis would call elder women in their clan "mother" and older men in their clan "mother's brother"; older men in their father's clan would be addressed as "father" and older women in their father's clan as "father's sister"; and older people called their younger clanmates "daughter" or "son." The Zuni used kinship terms for close friends as well. For example, people who were close childhood friends would call each other "brother" or "sister" and each other's parents "mother" and "father." Even certain natural forms merited kinship terms; the earth was "mother" and the sun "father." Rain clouds and fire were called "grandmother," water "grandfather," and corn either "sister" or "brother."

The Zuni formed bonds with nonrelatives through marriage. Married couples were expected to act as partners, cooperating in their work and helping to support each other's families. Most marriages succeeded, but if a couple did not get along well, either spouse was free to divorce the other (although the woman kept any children). If the man chose to divorce, he simply left his wife's household and returned to his mother's home. If the woman wanted to end the marriage, she put her husband's belongings outside the house, and the man took his possessions and left. But when the marriage succeeded, the bonds it established extended beyond the couple to include both sets of relatives, and children born to the couple could depend upon the members of their own household and their father's family (or, if their parents divorced, their stepfather's family) for support.

RAISING CHILDREN

Child rearing was not only the responsibility of the parents but also of the entire family. Grandparents were often especially indulgent of their grandchildren, instructing and entertaining them by recounting myths and histories. In addition, older siblings, both boys and girls, participated in the care of their younger sisters and brothers.

To an extent, the entire community was engaged in the raising of each child, because any passerby was considered free or even obligated to reprimand a misbehaving child. The importance of family and community was instilled in every Zuni child from birth. A child intimately knew his or her universe of relatives because they lived together, they cooperated in their endeavors, and they gave each other emotional support.

As Zuni children grew up, they gradually learned the tasks that would be required of them as adults. Boys would help their fathers in the fields by planting and weeding crops, while girls would learn to grind corn and would assist their mothers by tending to younger siblings. Zuni children were usually taught by example and encouragement, not by punishment; however, children who misbehaved frequently were sometimes told frightening stories about owls, witches, and certain kachinas who carried away naughty children. And if a mother was especially exasperated with her child, she would ask the chief of a kachina society to make sure a child-snatching kachina was present at the next public dance. When the kachina appeared at the dance, it would approach the offending child and menace him, saying that it was going to carry him off and eat him if he did not behave.

Although children might be scolded and corrected verbally, they were never punished physically. The Zuni attitude toward misbehavior was that the child did not know any better, not that the child was "bad" or "mean."

Ideally, Zuni girls and boys would grow up to be generous, helpful, considerate, and moderate people. The community strongly encouraged and valued these characteristics. Consequently, visitors to Zuni households were usually given a generous and hospitable welcome. According to Frank Cushing, a researcher who lived with the Zuni for several years in the late nineteenth century:

> The instant greeting to a Zuni house is "Enter, sit, and eat!" Enter any house at whatever time of day or night and the invariable tray of breads will be brought forth, also parched corn, or, if in the seasons, peaches, melons or piñon nuts.

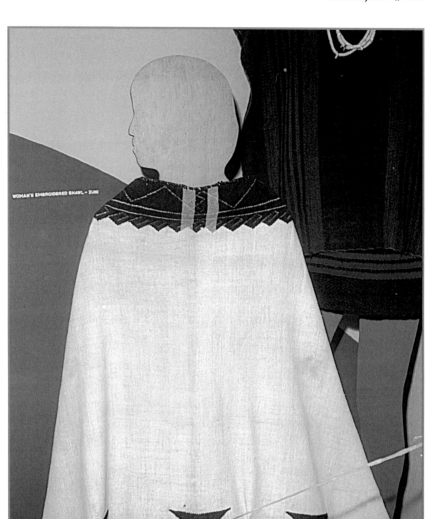

WOMAN'S EMBROIDERED SHAWL - ZUNI

Zuni clothing, such as this cape, was made from dyed animal hides or cotton. Local mines provided materials for jewelry, such as turquoise, silver, and copper.

The Zuni strongly disapproved of people who were boastful, argumentative, uncooperative, or stingy. According to Ruth Bunzel, an anthropologist who visited the Zuni from 1928 to 1933:

> In all social relations, whether within the family group or outside, the most honored personality traits are a pleasing address, a yielding disposition, and a generous heart. The person who thirsts for power, who wishes to be, as they scornfully phrase it, "a leader of the people," receives nothing but criticism.

Conflicts and public disagreements were discouraged. Disputes—even those involving fairly serious crimes—were supposed to be settled privately and quietly by the families of the people involved. If a person repeatedly acted in an unacceptable manner, the people in the community would make their disapproval obvious by publicly teasing the wrongdoer (this was often the duty of the ritual clowns) or gossiping about the person's actions to shame the wrongdoer into correcting his or her behavior. Repeated or serious misbehavior exposed a person to accusations of witchcraft, which could lead to ostracism from the tribe or, in extreme cases, execution.

ZUNI GOVERNMENT

The government of the Zuni consisted of a *pekwin,* who was the head secular authority, and a council of priests, who were responsible for managing collective work, community affairs, and religious ceremonies. Each village had its own pekwin and council. The council of priests named the pekwin and could remove him from office if the people disapproved of his behavior. To become a pekwin, a man had to have a generous and kind disposition and be respected by all; in addition, he had to be a member of the Dogwood clan. The pekwin was officially installed in office during a ceremony conducted by the village's head Rain Priest, who would place a staff made of feathers in the chief's hands, recite a prayer, and then blow on the staff four times.

The council of priests appointed a pekwin to govern because it believed that if the priests became directly involved in village disputes, they would no longer be pure of heart and their prayers would lose power. Priests nonetheless exercised a great deal of influence by setting moral examples and encouraging others to act properly. To help with the more practical problems of governance, the pekwin had two assistants who were warriors and members of the Bow Priesthood.

Thanks to a unique system of government, a thorough exploitation of the resources around them, and a social system that emphasized mutual support and cooperation, the Zuni created a smoothly functioning society that provided most individuals with lives of security and purpose. Even the Spanish conquistadores who came into Zuni territory in the mid-sixteenth century remarked on the orderliness and fellowship of Zuni society. One soldier, named Castañeda, wrote in 1540:

> They have priests who preach; these are aged men who ascend to the highest terrace of the village and deliver a sermon at sunrise. The people sit around and listen in profound silence. These old men give them advice in regard to their manner of living, which they think it their duty to observe; for there is no drunkenness among them, no unnatural vice; there are no thieves; on the contrary, they are very laborious.

The Zuni prospered through the centuries by developing their resources and living for the most part in harmony with the people around them. Their stability, however, was threatened in the sixteenth century when invaders from Spain came into the American Southwest looking for treasures and remained there to dominate the original inhabitants.

Defending
the Homeland

The Spanish invasion of the Southwest began in the middle years of the sixteenth century. The Spanish had defeated the rich Aztec Empire in central Mexico in 1521 and were seeking to extend their control over other, hopefully equally wealthy Native American tribes. Spanish explorers traveled through the northern provinces of Mexico, searching for cities filled with treasures, but they found only small groups of farmers, hunters, and gatherers. Eventually the explorers mounted expeditions into the territory of the Zuni and other Pueblo tribes. Accompanying these explorers were priests belonging to the Franciscan order of the Roman Catholic Church, who hoped to convert the Native Americans to Christianity.

In 1538 the viceroy of Mexico, Antonio de Mendoza, chose a Franciscan priest named Fray Marcos de Niza to lead a party into present-day New Mexico and Arizona. The viceroy wanted to gain subjects for the king of Spain and converts for the Catholic Church. He told Niza:

> You must explain to the natives of the land that there is only one God in heaven, and the Emperor on earth to rule and govern it, whose subjects they all must become and whom they must serve.

Marcos de Niza ventured into the American Southwest early in 1539, sending a small group in advance of the main contingent under the leadership of a Moor named Estevanico. Estevanico's party reached Zuni lands, but once they arrived, Estevanico gravely offended the tribe and was executed. His specific offense is not known—according to Zuni oral tradition, the "black Mexican" was "greedy, voracious and bold"—but some have speculated that he unwisely informed the Zuni of the size and military nature of the larger party that was to join him.

In any case, when word of Estevanico's death reached Niza, he quickly returned to Mexico and told Mendoza that he had found a kingdom richer even than the empire of the Aztecs. It is unclear whether Niza actually saw Hawikuh during his expedition; in any case, he wildly exaggerated its wealth, claiming that its houses were decorated with turquoise and other jewels. Niza also claimed that Hawikuh formed a part of a mighty empire called the Seven Cities of Cibola. For years to come, the Zuni's territory was known as Cibola (probably a corruption of the Zuni phrase *Shi-wi-na,* used to indicate any permanent Zuni town or residence) and the Zuni themselves as Cibolans. Niza's fertile imagination was reflected in his name for the Cibolan Empire; the Zuni probably inhabited only six villages at this time, but both Aztec and European legend mentioned wealthy empires encompassing seven cities, so Niza credited the Zuni with seven.

CORONADO'S EXPEDITION

Obviously, news of the Seven Cities of Cibola was quite welcome to Viceroy Mendoza, who sent a large force into the region to conquer the wealthy Cibolans and plunder their treasures. The expedition—consisting of 230 soldiers on horseback, 70 foot soldiers, several Franciscan priests, and hundreds of Mexican Indians—was led by Francisco Vásquez de Coronado. Coronado planned to force the Cibolans to submit to Spain's authority, while the Franciscans planned to establish missions and convert the empire of Cibola to Christianity.

The Zuni, of course, had their own plans. Expecting reprisals for the killing of Estevanico, the Zuni prepared for an attack at Hawikuh, evacuating all women, children, and elderly from the village onto nearby mesas. The Zuni made a preliminary attempt to drive off the Spanish by attacking them at a narrow canyon near the juncture of the Zuni and Little Colorado rivers, and they inflicted several casualties. But the Spanish continued toward Hawikuh, reaching an open plain south of the town in early July 1540. According to a Spanish officer, when the Spanish arrived at the plain, they "found all the Indians of Cibola and the people of other places who had gathered to meet us with force."

Six hundred Zuni warriors were assembled to turn back the Spanish invasion. At first the battle went well for the Zuni, who managed to repel the initial Spanish assault, but the superior weaponry of the Spanish helped turn the tide, and when the soldiers began a second attack against Hawikuh, the Zuni, suffering serious casualties, surrendered the town. Coronado, who had been injured in the battle, and his men occupied Hawikuh. The village proved to be somewhat disappointing to the Spanish: Most residents had fled, and Hawikuh lacked the lavish riches reported by Niza. The conquistadores were quite impressed with the Zuni's agricultural bounty, but they were in search of gold, not grain, and eventually left Zuni territory to investigate the villages of the Pueblo tribes along the Rio Grande. Several priests and soldiers stayed behind for another two years to assert Spanish authority in the region; they returned to Mexico in 1542, leaving two Mexican Indian converts to Christianity to spread the word among

Hoping to exploit the Zuni as they did the Aztec, a Spanish expedition attacked the Hawikuh settlement. Although the Zuni were anticipating the attack, their arrows were no match against Spanish guns, and they surrendered their city.

the Zuni. According to a Spanish officer who was a member of the party traveling to Mexico, after they left Hawikuh, "for two or three days, the Zunis never ceased to follow the rear guard of the army to pick up any baggage or Indian servants. . . . They rejoiced at keeping some of our people."

Although Zuni warriors harassed the party of priests and soldiers, the two Mexican Indians left behind were treated quite well, and according to later visitors to Hawikuh, they eventually recanted their Christianity and married into the tribe. This pattern was to be repeated throughout the period of Spanish conquest; the Zuni tradition of generosity and hospitality to strangers resulted in most visitors being treated quite well, but newcomers who tried to disrupt or interfere with traditional Zuni life were threatened, harassed, or killed.

An Explorer's Observations

During an expedition throughout Puebloan territory in 1582, Antonio de Espejo wrote about his observations of Native life. For example, he described their food, houses, methods of leadership, and some aspects of their beliefs as he interpreted them. Following are some excerpts from his accounts, according to *The Pueblo Indians of North America*:

> They grind raw corn on very large stones, five or six women working together, and from the flour they make many kinds of bread. Their houses are two, three, or four stories high, each house being partitioned into a number of rooms. In the pueblos each plaza has two "estufas" [kivas] which are houses built underground, well sheltered and tightly closed, with benches inside to sit on. At the entrance to each estufa there is a ladder for going down into it.
>
> Some of the natives are clad in cotton blankets, buffalo hides, or dressed chamois skins. They wear blankets, except that over their privy parts, they have small pieces of colored cotton cloth, and some of them wear shirts. The women have cotton skirts, often embroidered with colored

After Coronado left Zuni territory in 1540, he set up headquarters in the Pueblo village of Tiguex, located on the Rio Grande near present-day Bernalillo, New Mexico. From there, he sent expeditions to contact and to obtain tribute from other Pueblo villages, eventually exercising dominion over nearly all of the Rio Grande villages. The Zuni, however, were far to the west of the Rio Grande, and after Coronado's disappointment, the Spanish had little interest in exploiting their territory. As a result, for the next 40 years the Zuni had no recorded contact with the Spanish, although informal thread, and over the shoulders a blanket fastened at the waist by a strip of embroidered material, with tassels. The skirts are worn like slips common next to the skin. Everyone, man or woman, wears shoes or boots with soles of buffalo hide and uppers of dressed deerskin. They do not wear any head covering.

All of the pueblos have "caciques" [leaders] allotted according to the number of inhabitants. Thus there are principal caciques, who in turn have others under them, the latter functioning like sheriffs to execute the orders of their superiors.

In every one of these pueblos there is a house to which food is brought for the Devil. The natives have small stone idols which they worship; and also, just as the Spaniards have crosses along the roads, these people set up their artificial hillocks built of stones like wayside shrines, where they place painted sticks and feathers.

They have fields planted with corn, beans, calabashes, and tobacco in abundance. These crops are seasonal, dependent on rainfall. In each planted field the worker has a shelter, where food is carried to him at noon and he spends the siesta; for usually the workers stay in their fields from morning until night.

meetings might have occurred, and the Zuni almost certainly received information on Spanish activities through their trade with the Pueblo tribes who lived along the Rio Grande. Although the Zuni lived farther to the west, they were also a Pueblo tribe and shared many cultural features with the Rio Grande groups.

EXPEDITIONS CONTINUE

In 1581 the Spanish, in an attempt to expand their domain and investigate persistent rumors of incredible treasure to the west, sent an expedition into Zuni territory led by Francisco Sánchez Chamuscado, but the only riches he found were agricultural. Two years later, Antonio de Espejo led a contingent to the Zuni village of Matsaki, looking for copper and silver mines. He failed to find the mines and soon departed from the area, but he left behind several soldiers and priests to codify Spanish control.

As with Coronado, the Zuni benefited immensely in their dealings with Espejo by being in an out-of-the-way location that was not believed to contain anything of great value. Espejo and his soldiers routinely demanded vast quantities of food and cloth-ing from the Pueblo Indians who lived along the Rio Grande, and they usually slaughtered the inhabitants of any village that defied them. Because of their location, however, the Zuni escaped much of this mistreatment, but the combination of deference and defen-sive preparation that marked their future relations with the Span-ish strongly indicates that they had heard tales of the repeated atrocities.

THE COLONY OF NEW MEXICO

In 1598, the Spanish government established a permanent colony of settlers in what was called New Mexico and named Juan de Oñate as the first governor of the colony. Oñate was determined to exploit both the human and mineral resources of the colony, and that year he traveled to the Zuni's territory to order their leaders to declare their obedience to the Spanish king and to explore their territory for valuable natural resources. Of special interest to Oñate were the rumored copper mines of the Zuni and Zuni Salt Lake, which could provide settlers with a popular seasoning and pre-servative. Oñate sent two parties of soldiers to explore and assess these potential sources of wealth. The soldiers sent to the mines reported that they had indeed found mines of great antiquity, but they were vague as to the location and the potential value of the excavations. The soldiers sent to Zuni Salt Lake had more encour-aging news, reporting that the lake had a crust of salt on it so thick that a man could walk on it, and they brought back a sample of salt that Oñate declared superior to any found in Europe.

Oñate hardly left the area encouraged, however. As useful as a salt lake might be for supporting a settlement, it was hardly the literal gold mine he had hoped to find. Oñate's search for exploitable resources reached a head as complaints about his conduct led to threats that he would lose the governorship of New Mexico. He visited Zuni territory again in 1604, looking for the copper mines his men had supposedly located on the earlier expedition. A Spanish official who accompanied the expedition noted that four of the six Zuni villages were "almost completely in ruins," a fact that probably reflects the toll taken by European diseases, as well as the migrations caused by intermittent conflicts with passing Spanish soldiers. European diseases that had never before been experienced in North America had devastating effects in Native communities.

Oñate's second search for the Zuni mines was a failure, and in 1607 authorities in Mexico removed him as governor of the colony and replaced him with Pedro de Peralta, who arrived in 1609 and established a provincial capital in the village of Santa Fe. Peralta, however, continued the abusive policies of his predecessors, exacting forced labor and tribute from the Rio Grande Pueblo Indians. The Franciscan missionaries also became quite powerful during this period and were equally brutal in their exploitation of the Native Americans. Missionaries forced the Pueblo Indians to work in their fields and homes, to build churches and houses in their villages, and to attend church services. In addition, many missionaries destroyed non-Christian ceremonial objects and religious works of art, and they punished defiant or uncooperative Native Americans with public whippings, tortures, and executions. Native Americans who practiced their traditional religions were often viciously persecuted for practicing witchcraft, a crime defined by the Spanish as any exercise of non-Christian religious activities.

Once again, the location of the Zuni settlements allowed them to escape some of the more intense forms of control, but their experience with the missionaries was negative enough that Spanish-speaking Catholics were banned from Zuni rituals and dances well into the twentieth century. The missionaries to the Zuni usually served a large area and never stayed long in any one village. As a result, the Zuni would usually abstain from their public religious ceremonies when a missionary was in town, then continue as usual once the missionary left.

The Zuni were no more cooperative with the secular Spanish authorities. They were expected to pay tribute and to perform work for the Spaniards, including farmwork and the gathering of piñon nuts, which officials sold for huge profits in Mexico. The Spanish soon discovered, however, that the Zuni would only pay tribute when threatened by an armed force, an expensive, tiresome, and not altogether safe way to make collections. Officials in Santa Fe eventually gave up on collecting tribute from the Zuni after 1621.

MISSIONARIES IN ZUNI TERRITORY

Eventually, though, the Spanish tried to reassert control over the Zuni. In the late 1620s, an officer named Silva Nieto led a contingent of 30 soldiers and several priests into Zuni lands. Nieto demanded that the people submit to Spanish authority, but the Zuni, led by their council of religious elders, refused. Nieto departed but left two Franciscan priests to establish a mission in the village of Hawikuh. The presence of the priests was an immediate source of conflict, and Nieto had to return with his soldiers a few days later to menace the Zuni into accepting them.

The priests—the first permanent resident missionaries in Zuni territory—were quick to begin what they considered the work of God. Using Zuni labor, they oversaw the construction of a mission compound in Hawikuh, which contained a massive church with a nave measuring 103 by 20 feet (31 by 6 meters), as well as a kitchen, a chapel, residences, and workrooms. The compound was completed in 1632, and a second mission was established in the town of Halona around the same time.

The Franciscan missionaries might have felt optimistic, but they had seriously underestimated the resentment caused by their use of Zuni labor and their interference with Zuni religious life. This resentment worsened after a new priest—a blunt, opinionated, and unpopular man—arrived in Hawikuh determined to stamp out the Zuni religion. Shortly after the compounds were built, the new priest tried to interfere with a Zuni ceremony and force those in attendance to go to Mass instead. The Zuni, infuriated at his audacity, killed him and another priest who was passing through the area and destroyed the missions. The other resident priests immediately vacated the territory, and officials in Santa Fe sent soldiers to punish the people responsible.

By the time the soldiers reached the villages, however, the Zuni had abandoned them and settled in a large community on top of an easily defendable mesa called Dowa Yalanne, or Corn Mountain. The Zuni eventually allowed some missionaries accompanying the soldiers into their new village to negotiate a settlement. The Zuni promised to accept the authority of the Spanish crown, and the Spanish promised to allow the Zuni to return to their villages. The soldiers left the region, but the cautious Zuni remained on Dowa Yalanne for another three years before returning to their old villages.

The lack of Spanish documentation concerning the Zuni from 1632 to 1680 seems to indicate that authorities made few additional attempts to control them at this time, although informal contact almost surely continued. A few missionaries took up residence in Zuni towns and tried, with little success, to have the Zuni rebuild the missions. The missionaries did have some impact on Zuni life, however; when the Zuni publicly performed their traditional religious dances and ceremonies, the priests reportedly arrested a number of religious leaders and punished them with public beatings, confiscated ritual objects, and burned kivas.

The Zuni abandoned their custom of hospitality whenever foreigners interfered with their traditions or religion. After murdering a Spanish missionary for interrupting a religious ritual, the Zuni left their villages and hid from the Spanish military on Dowa Yalanne, or Corn Mountain, *(above)* for three years.

Despite what was surely bad blood between the missionaries and the Zuni, only one missionary was reported to have been murdered during this period, and he was apparently the victim of Navajo or Apache raiders.

Spanish domination of the Zuni may have been less intense than in other Puebloan communities, but their presence and influence did have critical consequences in Zuni society. For example, archaeological evidence suggests that by 1680, Zuni women were no longer occupying important community leadership positions as they had in previous times. This evidence comes from the examination of burials in the major Zuni center of Hawikuh, occupied from about 1350 to 1680. Grave goods buried with the dead can be used to analyze leadership roles based on the amount and the diversity of artifacts found in the graves. In times prior to Spanish influence at the beginning of the seventeenth century, men and women filled leadership roles, consistent with Zuni principles of gender equality. By the middle of the seventeenth century, however, women were excluded from community leadership positions. A major shift occurred that favored men, particularly as warriors and defenders of the villages. The roles of warriors gained prominence because of the need to defend the communities against Spanish invaders and attacks carried out by Apache and Navajo raiders, who increasingly targeted the settled Puebloan towns.

In addition, Spanish political offices instituted in Puebloan villages in the seventeenth century were open only to men, further marginalizing women leaders. Finally, the European concepts of gender preached by Franciscan missionaries favored the household and community leadership of men, restricting public roles for women.

THE PUEBLO REVOLT

For many reasons, resentment ran high against the Spanish even though their presence in Zuni settlements was intermittent. In 1680, the Zuni joined a Pueblo Indian rebellion, led by a Tewa named Popé, to oust the Spanish officials, soldiers, priests, and settlers from the Southwest. Popé and the other leaders planned a siege of the provincial capital of Santa Fe. They decided to start their rebellion in the summer, just before an annual delivery of supplies from Mexico, when the Spanish would have the fewest guns and ammunition. The date of the rebellion was set for August 11, 1680, and two messengers were chosen to convey details of the planned uprising to all the Pueblo tribes. But the Spanish governor, Antonio de Otermin, found out about the impending revolt and arrested the two messengers on August 9. When word of the arrests spread in the villages, the leaders decided to begin the rebellion immediately. The Pueblo Revolt began on August 10, when the inhabitants of the Rio Grande villages cut off water and supplies to Santa Fe, and by August 21 all Spanish troops and settlers had left the Southwest.

The Zuni carried out their part of the Pueblo Revolt by killing the resident priest of Halona (according to Zuni oral tradition, another priest was allowed to live because he disavowed his Christianity and became a Zuni), burning the church buildings that they had been forced to build, and expelling Spanish settlers who had intruded on their land. As a defensive measure, the Zuni once again abandoned their villages and moved to a settlement on top of Dowa Yalanne, where they remained for more than 15 years.

In 1692, a Spanish commander named Diego de Vargas led a large force of soldiers from Mexico into Pueblo territory and regained control of most of the towns along the Rio Grande. Vargas traveled west to reconquer the Hopi and the Zuni. When he reached Dowa Yalanne, he was received with surprising cordiality by the Zuni. Although Zuni leaders had met with representatives from the nearby Hopi and Keres to plan a united defense against the Spanish, the size of the Spanish force that reached Dowa Yalanne probably compelled the Zuni leadership to offer instead to live in peace with the intruders. In addition, after the Pueblo Revolt the Zuni had had increasing trouble with raiders from other Native American tribes. The introduction of the horse to America had made the formerly peaceful Navajo and Apache fearsome foes who could raid a farm, steal crops, livestock, and people, and escape with lightning speed. Comanche and Ute raiders had also moved into the area. The powerful Spanish military probably enticed the Zuni to become allies with them against the raiders.

The Zuni, however, had not completely capitulated to the Spanish. When, in 1694, another Spanish contingent approached Dowa Yalanne seeking tribute and oaths of obedience, the Zuni successfully fought off the soldiers, inflicting many casualties and causing the army to retreat quickly to Santa Fe. This successful resistance led to rumors in Santa Fe that the Zuni and their allies among the Hopi, Keres, and Apache planned to attack Spanish settlements. Missionaries added to the tension by complaining that the Zuni refused to convert to Christianity. The missionaries finally requested that Diego de Vargas, the governor at Santa Fe, send soldiers against the Zuni, but Vargas believed the rumors to be false and denied the request. The armed uprising never materialized.

The Spanish nonetheless continued to seek obedience from the Zuni. In 1699, a new governor, Pedro Rodríguez Cubero, sent a delegation to Dowa Yalanne to have the Zuni renew earlier pledges of peace. The meeting seems to have gone fairly well, for shortly after the Spanish delegation left, the Zuni finally moved down from their defensive settlement on Dowa Yalanne. The threat of attacks from Indian raiders and the Spanish still existed, however, and the Zuni concentrated their population in Halona (later called Zuni by English-speaking Americans), on the assumption that it would be easier to defend one large village than several small settlements scattered over a wide area.

As the defensive design of Halona suggests, the Zuni were far from being conquered or even reconquered, even though they had agreed not to fight the Spanish. Despite tremendous pressure from their would-be conquistadores, the Zuni never acquiesced to foreign control of their government, and at the end of the seventeenth century, they remained a free and independent people. This independence, however, was to come under further attack during the next two centuries from Spanish, Mexican, and then U.S. dominance.

Aliens on
Native Soil

As the eighteenth century began, the Spanish continued their attempts to increase their authority over the Pueblo Indians. Although they were able to govern the people living in villages along the Rio Grande with relative ease, they had difficulty controlling the Zuni. Since the Zuni lived far from Santa Fe, officials found it too costly to continually send troops to force them to comply with Spanish laws. The Zuni's isolation from the Spanish domain was aided by the fact that the Navajo and Apache inhabited the territory between the Zuni and the Rio Grande. These tribes routinely raided soldiers on the march, and Spanish officials quickly became reluctant to risk troops and supplies by sending them through this dangerous territory to the Zuni.

On the rare occasions that the Spanish visited the Zuni, the Zuni leaders would readily promise to live in peace with the Spanish, to follow Spanish law, to attend Catholic services, and to give up their traditional religious practices. As soon as the authorities returned to Santa Fe, however, the Zuni would ignore all requests for tribute and resume their religious practices. As a result, of the three missions built in Zuni villages by the middle of the seventeenth century, only one, a church at Halona, was rebuilt after the reconquest, and it was seldom used.

Not surprisingly, Franciscan missionaries made only a few permanent converts among the Zuni and other Pueblo Indians. Indeed, although missionaries became a regular sight in Halona, they were usually visiting from other Pueblo villages and more frequently acted as diplomats rather than as religious leaders. In 1776, a priest named Fray Dominguez wrote about the mission's lack of success:

> Even at the end of so many years since the reconquest, . . . their condition now is almost the same as it was in the beginning, for generally speaking they have preserved some very indecent, and perhaps superstitious customs.
>
> Their repugnance and resistance to most Christian acts is evident, for they perform the duties pertaining to the Church under compulsion, and there are usually many omissions.

Friction between Spanish civil and religious authorities also helped the Zuni maintain their isolation and independence. Civilian officials often complained about the lack of progress made by Franciscans among the Pueblo Indians and noted the priests' abusive and illegal practices. Juan Antonio de Ornedal y Masa, an envoy of the Spanish viceroy, listed several improprieties:

> The religious almost totally neglect the Indians, even failing to say Mass for them. The missionaries, in violation of the law, fail to learn the Native language and to teach the Indians the Spanish language. The missionaries forcibly take grain and sheep from the Indians who are also compelled to weave for them wool and cotton without pay. They arbitrarily take from the Indians buffalo skins that they obtain for sheltering themselves and the buckskins that they sell. When the Indians complain of this to

Because the Zuni lived farther west than the surrounding tribes, the Spanish found it difficult to exert control or establish an influence. Spanish priests built churches *(above)*, but few Zuni converted to Christianity, and soon all missionary activity ceased among the Zuni.

the civil authorities, the priests threaten them with whippings and other punishments.

For their part, missionaries repeatedly wrote to the viceroy and recounted abuses by civil authorities against the Pueblo Indians. In 1761, Fray Pedro Serrano complained that officials forced men, women, and children to weave blankets, harvest corn, and perform domestic work. Serrano ended his letter by observing that:

These officials never conduct themselves in any way that yields any benefit to the Indians. . . . We religious suffer many injuries, outrages, and afflictions from the officials if we try to defend the unfortunate Indians in any way. . . . The officials laugh, for they alone are favored and protected [knowing that] the best officials are those who oppress the Indians most.

As a result of the bickering, resistance, and general lack of success, the Franciscans had all but stopped their missionary activity among the Zuni when they were officially recalled by the newly formed Mexican government in 1821.

COOPERATION

Although the Zuni never abandoned their own religious and cultural practices, the Zuni and the Spanish did cooperate in some areas. The Zuni generally accepted the presence of priests in their towns and, in keeping with their traditional ideal of generous hospitality toward strangers, they even warmly welcomed missionaries and other Spanish visitors. If the newcomers' actions violated Zuni norms, however, the offenders were dealt with decisively. For example, in 1700 a group of Spanish soldiers, accompanied by a missionary and three Spanish settlers, were welcomed into Halona to defend the village against raiders. The troops and settlers, though, treated the Zuni with disdain and curtness, and behaved licentiously (inappropriately) toward the Zuni women. On March 3, 1703, the Zuni decided that they had had enough and killed the three settlers, sparing the missionary because he had behaved well and the soldiers only because they were absent from town that day. The Zuni believed they would be punished for the killings and quickly evacuated once again to Dowa Yalanne, but the Spanish had decided by this point that the survival of their colonists depended upon the cultivation of goodwill among the Pueblo Indians. Consequently, the Spanish expedition sent to Dowa Yalanne two years later was led by the spared missionary, who made an agreement with the Zuni promising them clemency and military protection. The Zuni promptly moved back to Halona and even sent delegates to a 1706 meeting in Santa Fe between the new Spanish governor and representatives of all the Pueblo tribes (except the militantly anti-Spanish Hopi, who eventually engaged in some minor conflicts with the Zuni because of the latter's cooperation with the Spanish).

After the 1705 agreement, the Zuni even engaged in a temporary military alliance with the Spanish. Throughout the eighteenth century, the Navajo and the Apache carried out several attacks against Halona, with casualties resulting on both sides. In retaliation, Zuni warriors sometimes joined Spanish soldiers in expeditions against the Navajo and the Apache. These joint actions did not, however, create a lasting alliance or bond between the Zuni and the Spanish but were rather merely a temporary expedience for the beleaguered and vengeful Zuni. Indeed, by the late eighteenth century, Spanish authorities had given up hope of dominating the Zuni and other western Pueblo Indians, and in 1799 only seven Spanish people were recorded as living among the Zuni. Spanish rule in all of the American Southwest finally ended in 1821, when the nation of Mexico won its independence from Spain.

THE ZUNI AND OTHER TRIBES

The Zuni's relationships with many of their Native neighbors were most often friendly and productive. Members of many tribes visited one another, traded with each other, and intermarried. Trade took place locally and informally but also occurred in the context of large, intertribal trading fairs. At these fairs, people from many tribes exchanged goods, met and socialized, and learned from each other.

Although the Zunis had remained mostly independent during the period of Spanish domination, contact with these foreigners had affected their lives in several important ways. They adopted numerous articles of European manufacture, such as metal knives, axes, saws, scissors, nails, pots, and kettles. These metal implements and utensils were more durable than traditional wooden, bone, or clay items.

At a Trading Fair

Intertribal trade fairs brought together people from many Native nations. The following, from *The Pueblo Indians of North America,* is a description of one such fair that occurred in 1776 at the pueblo of Taos in New Mexico, recorded by Father Dominguez, a Spanish cleric:

> At this fair, they sell buffalo hides, white elkskins, horse, mules, buffalo meat. They also sell good guns, pistols, powder, tobacco, hatchets, and some vessels of yellow tin. These have a handle made of an iron hoop to carry them. The Comanches acquire these articles from the Wichitas who have direct communication and trade with the French, from whom they buy them. The Comanche usually sell to our people at this rate: a buffalo hide for a broad knife made entirely of iron; a white elkskin for a very poor bridle; the meat for maize or corn flour. If they sell a she-mule, either a cover or a short cloak or a good horse is given; if they sell a horse, a poor bridle, but garnished with red rags is given for it; if they sell a pistol, its price is a bridle.
>
> They are great traders, for as soon as they buy anything, they usually sell exactly what they bought, and usually they keep losing. In short, the trading day resembles a second-hand market in Mexico, the way people mill about.

The Spanish also introduced a number of new crops to the Zuni. These crops, which had been brought from Europe or Mexico, included wheat, oats, peaches, apples, melons, tomatoes, and chili. In addition, the Spanish introduced the Zuni to sheep and burros, animals that would greatly alter the Zuni economy. Burros were useful as pack animals, while sheep were valuable sources of meat and wool. Zuni women spun the wool into yarn and wove it into blankets and clothing, which were sold to Spanish and Mexican traders.

An indirect but profound result of the Spanish invasion was a change in Zuni settlement patterns. Before 1540, the Zuni resided in six villages along the Zuni River, but by the end of the seventeenth century, all but one of these villages, Halona (later Zuni), had been abandoned. Because of the large increase in population in this village, a great deal of new housing was constructed. Rooms were added to existing houses, and new homes were built on hills facing the Zuni River, as well as on flat ground at the edge of the village.

Because of the circumstances under which Halona expanded, the new buildings changed the village's design so that it was better suited for military defense. The large, multistoried houses all faced inward around central plazas, which were only accessible through a few narrow passages. Rooms on the ground floor usually had no doors or windows, and to enter a house, a person had to climb a ladder onto the rooftop and then climb down another ladder through an entrance in the roof. If intruders approached the village, the ladders to the rooftops could be pulled up, barring access to the rooms and their inhabitants below.

The crops and animals introduced by the Spanish also affected settlement patterns. Once people owned large numbers of sheep, they needed to devote a good deal of time to grazing the animals and had to turn part of their land into pasture. At the same time, the introduction of the burro meant that fairly large amounts of produce or supplies could be easily carried long distances from a field to the village or vice versa. As a result of these two developments, the Zuni established several small farming communities and herding camps a substantial distance from Halona in the early eighteenth century. At first, these communities and camps were inhabited only during the summer, but three communities became permanent later in the century. The village farthest from Halona was called Nutria (or *toya* in Zuni) and was located 25 miles (40 kilometers) northeast of Halona along the Nutria

Sheep, burros, and new Spanish crops drastically changed the Zuni way of life. Shepherds and farmers needed more land and lived away from the larger community, while those who lived inside Halona adapted their homes to prevent intruders.

River. Ojo Caliente (or *kapkwayina,* meaning "water comes up from the depths") was established 15 miles (24 kilometers) to the southwest of Halona, and Pescado (or *heshota cina,* meaning "marked house") was situated east of Halona on the Pescado River.

Yet another change that occurred during the period of Spanish influence was the establishment of civilian government in Zuni villages. Before the Spanish invasion, religious leaders governed the towns through their appointment of a pekwin. After the reconquest of 1692, the Spanish set up a council of civil authorities that operated as a parallel council to the traditional leadership, which retained control over religious and moral matters. The civilian government included a governor, a lieutenant governor, and a village council. At first, the Spanish appointed the head of the Bow Priesthood as governor, but by the middle of the nineteenth century, Zuni religious leaders chose the governor, lieutenant governor, and councillors. Although civilian and religious leaders had separate duties, they were installed in office through similar ceremonies. The head of the Rain Priesthood installed the traditional pekwin and also gave the oath of office to the civilian governor. And just as the pekwin received a ceremonial staff of feathers as a symbol of his office, the civilian governor was given a wooden cane as his symbol of office.

Finally, a tragic result of contact between the Zuni and the Spanish was the introduction of deadly diseases of European origin. Before Europeans arrived in North America, the organisms that cause smallpox, measles, and influenza did not exist on the continent. Since the Zuni and other Native Americans had never been exposed to these diseases, they had not developed any natural resistance or immunities to them. Consequently, when the organisms were brought to America by the Europeans, they spread quickly and with deadly force among the vulnerable indigenous population.

Throughout North America, millions of Native Americans died during widespread epidemics that erupted soon after contact with Europeans. The Zuni were no exception, and several devastating epidemics of smallpox and measles struck Zuni communities in the sixteenth and seventeenth centuries. Although population figures for the early years of the Spanish invasion are not completely reliable, the Zuni population might have been as high as 10,000 in the mid-sixteenth century. By the time of the Pueblo Revolt in 1680, their population had declined to 2,500. The population continued to decrease, and by the end of the eighteenth century, the Zuni numbered only 1,600. Their population did not begin to increase again until late in the nineteenth century.

UNDER MEXICO

When the Spanish left the Southwest in 1821, the Mexican government assumed jurisdiction over the region. The government declared that Native Americans were full citizens of Mexico and that their rights as citizens would be protected. The Mexican authorities, though, had no effective contact with the Zuni and other Pueblo Indians, who lived in what was then a marginal, outlying province of a new nation. This proved beneficial to the Zuni, who were able to practice their traditions free from official interference or harassment.

Even before the Mexican government gained control in the Southwest, however, intruders from the United States had begun to enter Zuni territory. A Creole trader named Jean Baptiste Lalande arrived in the Southwest in 1804, followed in 1821 by William Becknell, who set up trading operations in Santa Fe. Shortly afterward, American fur trappers entered the region, purchasing food and supplies from the Native Americans. Such commerce between Mexican citizens and foreigners was illegal under Mexican law, but American merchants, attracted to Halona's reputation as a center for intertribal trade, tried to establish trade networks with the Zuni. But because the Americans were primarily interested in valuable beaver furs and the supply of beavers in the Southwest was very small, trade between the Zuni and the Americans was not particularly profitable. By 1835, most American traders had left the region.

U.S.-MEXICAN WAR

Mexican jurisdiction over the Southwest was threatened with the outbreak of the U.S.-Mexican War in 1846. Besides fighting the Mexicans, U.S. troops in the Southwest fought a number of battles with Navajo raiders. In 1846, while in pursuit of some Navajo horse thieves, a group of about 60 U.S. soldiers happened upon Zuni Pueblo. The Zuni were delighted to find a common enemy of the Navajo, and the tribe fed and housed the soldiers in a most congenial manner. A report of the encounter between the Zuni and the Americans, written by a private in the army unit involved, noted:

> As soon as our horses were unsaddled, [the Zuni] furnished us with a house, and took us all off to different houses to eat. I went to one house where they set out a soup made with mutton and various kinds of vegetables, and a kind of bread as thin as paper. They have the reputation of being the most hospitable people in the world, which I believe they merit in every respect.
>
> We were out of provisions and proposed to buy from them, but they said they did not sell their provisions and more particularly to Americans. So they brought in sufficient bread and meal to last our party into camp, which is three days from here. Our saddles, bridles, and all equipment was left exposed to them, but in the morning, not a single article was gone. Where can such a mass of honest people be found?

The cordial meeting climaxed with an exchange of official pledges of peace and friendship between the U.S. Army officers and the Zuni governor Lai-iu-ah-tsai-ah.

The U.S.-Mexican War ended with Mexico's defeat in 1848. The Treaty of Guadalupe Hidalgo, signed by both countries after the war, granted the United States possession of the present-day states of New Mexico and Arizona. The treaty also contained a clause in which the U.S. government promised to respect the land and rights of the indigenous inhabitants of its new possession. That same year, Lai-iu-ah-tsai-ah and other Zuni leaders met with Navajo leaders and U.S. Army Lieutenant Colonel Henderson P. Boyakin to sign a three-way peace treaty. The treaty stated in part that the Zuni "shall be protected in the full management of all their rights of Private Property and Religion . . . [by] the authorities, civil and military, of New Mexico and the United States."

By the middle of the nineteenth century, the Zuni had been exposed to three foreign governments, each with its own plans for the indigenous peoples. Despite the turnover in outside powers, the Zuni had managed to maintain their own security and continue their traditional way of living, and when faced with a new would-be overlord, they had obtained treaties and agreements that explicitly protected their rights and properties. But the government, people, and traditions of the United States would put entirely new pressures on Zuni society, pressures that no treaty could contain.

Losses and Recoveries

One year after the United States signed a treaty with the Zuni, the superintendent of Indian affairs for the area, James Calhoun, visited the tribe. Calhoun expressed his desire to maintain friendly relations with the Zuni, and the Zuni leaders expressed their hope of living in peace. The friendly relations between the two governments were further cemented in 1863, when President Abraham Lincoln presented Zuni Pueblo governor Mariano with a silver-knobbed ebony cane, which thereafter became the ceremonial cane of office.

Relations, though, were far from ideal. The discovery of gold in California in 1848 brought a stream of travelers across Zuni lands. Most of these people were just passing through on their way to California, but some of them stole crops and livestock from Zuni farms. In addition, a number of people stayed in the region, enough so that the U.S. Congress organized the area as the Territory of New Mexico in 1850.

EXPEDITIONS INTO ZUNI TERRITORY

The 1850s also saw the U.S. government send several expeditions of scientists and technicians to conduct geographic surveys of New Mexico. A researcher named Baldwin Mollhausen described the Zuni's prosperity at the time. He wrote:

> They breed sheep, keep horses and asses, and practice agriculture on an extensive scale. In all directions, fields of wheat and maize, as well as gourds and melons, bore testimony to their industry. In gardens, they raise beans and onions. And the women are skillful in the art of weaving, and manufacture durable blankets.

These expeditions were not sent out to observe the Zuni, however, but to find feasible land routes to California. A road linking New Mexico with Southern California was quickly built, and it passed near Zuni; since the towns and forts that sprang up near the tribe were the first American settlements of any size east of Los Angeles, the Zuni began to see more and more travelers stop in the area to get provisions.

The U.S. government did send other expeditions for the sole purpose of gathering information about the Zuni and other Pueblo Indians. Beginning in the 1870s, the U.S. Bureau of American Ethnology sent teams to contact Native Americans in the region and study their societies. The writings of these ethnologists garnered a great deal of national attention, and as a result, increasing numbers of white American tourists began to visit Zuni territory. But the American ethnologists did not simply write about the Zuni; they also took material artifacts of Zuni culture, such as pots, prayer sticks, and masks, to send or sell to museums. The sheer scale of some of these collecting expeditions—in 1881 one team alone shipped more than 3,700 items of Zuni manufacture and more than 3,000 items of Hopi manufacture to the Smithsonian Institution in Washington, D.C.—rendered them comparable to the early Spanish tribute-collecting expeditions. Some items were

After gold was discovered in California, the U.S. government sent out expeditions to explore the area and to acquaint themselves with the local Native American groups. Their published descriptions of the Zuni and their pueblo homes triggered an increasing number of tourist visits to the region.

purchased from willing sellers, but many were sacred items that were simply seized or stolen from the tribe. These actions were to become major issues for the Zuni in the middle and later years of the twentieth century.

During the 1870s, increasing numbers of American missionaries arrived to try to convert the Zuni to various sects of Christianity. A group of Mormon missionaries founded a permanent settlement on the boundary of Zuni territory in 1876, and in response the Presbyterians built a mission and school just north of Zuni the following year. Neither sect met with much success: During this time, Mormons were viewed with suspicion and hostility by U.S. authorities, who actively discouraged the Zuni from becoming Mormon, and few Zuni parents wanted the foreigners at the Presbyterian school to supervise their children's education (although attendance increased somewhat after the Presbyterians began to pass out free lunches to the pupils). The missionaries were all quite vocal in condemning traditional Zuni religious beliefs and practices, and they frequently demanded that the U.S. government outlaw traditional rituals, much to the consternation of the tribe. Zuni religious practices were ultimately not made illegal, but the Zuni began to conduct formerly public ceremonies in private to avoid such censure.

Naturally, American traders accompanied the large flow of people. During the 1870s, three white American and two Native American traders established operations at Zuni. At first, trade was fairly limited, and the traders exchanged manufactured goods for traditional items, such as agricultural produce, cloth, jewelry, and pottery. Commerce expanded after 1881, however, when the Atlantic and Pacific Railroad completed a track to Gallup, New Mexico, 40 miles (64 kilometers) northeast of Zuni. Once the railroad opened, traders began to purchase sheep and cattle to ship by railroad to national markets in eastern and western states. As a result, the Zuni began to raise more herds, which they sold for cash that they used to buy American products.

CREATION OF THE RESERVATION

While the Zuni were increasing their livestock holdings, American sheepherders and cattle ranchers entered the Southwest looking for grazing pasture. A steady influx of settlers who encroached on Zuni territory led to increased hostility and competition between the Zuni and the outsiders. As more settlers arrived, the Zuni demanded that the U.S. government fulfill its obligations under the Treaty of Guadalupe Hidalgo to protect their land. Problems arose immediately because the exact extent of Zuni territory had never been properly surveyed and registered with the U.S.

A Visit to the East

In 1882 and again in 1886, five Zuni leaders took a trip to several eastern cities in the United States. They wanted to visit places that they had heard of and see where the white people who were surrounding their lands in New Mexico had come from. They had also heard stories of the eastern ocean (the Atlantic) and wanted to see its great expanse and to take back some water from what they called the "Ocean of the Sunrise." This name had great symbolic significance for them because of the sacredness of water to a people inhabiting arid lands and because of the spiritual meaning of the eastern direction, the direction of the sun and its powerful life-giving energy.

On their first trip, the Zuni toured Washington, D.C., where they met President Chester A. Arthur, and then went by train to Boston, passing through Baltimore and Philadelphia. On their second visit in 1886, the Zuni were invited to spend several months in Massachusetts near the Atlantic coast. Anthropologist Frank Cushing, who lived for many years among the Zuni, arranged both trips and accompanied the Zuni leaders. Besides helping his Zuni hosts, Cushing wanted to raise funds to carry out extensive archaeological and anthropological expeditions to the Southwest.

The sights and sounds of the large American cities impressed the Zuni visitors, who witnessed firsthand the dominant power and wealth of the United States. They reflected on the personalities and the values of American culture. In

government. In 1877, when President Rutherford B. Hayes issued an executive order to create the Zuni Reservation, the area of land within its boundaries was only about one-tenth the size of the territory the Zuni had traditionally occupied. Many landmarks particular, they voiced amazement at Americans' desire for other people's land and their individual competitiveness. These traits of greed and envy violated basic Zuni ethics that stressed cooperation and hospitality. In the words of Heluta, one of the Zuni travelers, as cited in *Zuni: Selected Writings of Frank Hamilton Cushing*:

> Such indeed are the Americans. Though we Indians live in a poor and dried-up country, though we may love them not, yet they gather around us and come into our country continually, and even strive to get our land from us. Is it possible for anyone to say what they want? Where is there a country more beautiful than this we are sitting in now? Is there any water needed here? Without irrigation, things grow green, and there is water to drink. . . . But the sentiment of home affects them not; the little bits of land they may own, or the house they may have been bred in, are as nothing to them: for they wander incessantly, wander through all difficulties and dangers, to seek new places and better things. Why is it they are so unceasingly unsatisfied?

> Another Zuni visitor, Palowahtiwa, responded, "Above every people they are a people of emulation, a people of fierce jealousies. . . . And if one American goes one day's journey in the direction of a difficult trail, it is not long ere another American will go two days' journey in the direction of a more difficult one. One American cannot bear that another shall surpass him."

and areas considered sacred to the Zuni were not included in the reservation, and many Zuni felt no particular obligation to quit using land they had always regarded as their own because of a proclamation made in some far-off city to the east.

Because of a surveying error, the reservation's borders also did not include several of the Zuni's small farming settlements, among them the village of Nutria and its nearby springs, which were vital to Zuni agriculture. A group of U.S. Army officers stationed at nearby Fort Wingate had earlier set up a ranch just east of the borders of Zuni territory called the Cibola Cattle Company. When they discovered the surveying error, the officers (who were infamous among the Zuni for illegally grazing their cattle on reservation lands) attempted to gain title to Nutria and its springs. One officer was the son-in-law of a powerful Illinois senator and presidential hopeful named John Logan, who on a tour of the Southwest had told the officers of the opportunity to obtain the valuable land. The eastern newspapers were tipped off to the affair by Frank Cushing, a researcher sent by the Bureau of American Ethnology and an adopted Zuni; the result was a tremendous scandal that pitted Logan's vociferous political supporters against his equally vocal opponents. An early casualty of this battle was Cushing, who was forced to leave the region by Logan in 1884. (Cushing would later return and continued his entire life to speak out on behalf of the Zuni.)

Fortunately for the Zuni, Senator Logan's landgrab occurred when the tribe actually exercised considerable influence in the East. The Zuni had been the subject of many a flattering popular book and magazine article, beginning with the memoirs of the soldiers the Zuni had hosted during the U.S.-Mexican War, and had captured the interest and sympathy of many white Americans. In addition, Cushing had arranged a well-publicized tour of the eastern states for several Zuni leaders in 1882. The party traveled to Chicago, Boston, and Washington, D.C., meeting President Chester A. Arthur and a number of other highly prominent intellectual and business leaders. The tribal leaders impressed many of these influential easterners, who became advocates of Zuni land protection; as a result of their efforts, a second executive order was issued in 1883 that added the outlying farm areas, including Nutria and its springs, to the reservation area. A later trip made in 1886 by the Zuni governor and two of his aides helped further publicize the Zuni cause.

ENCROACHING ON THE LAND

But tours of eastern cities did not prevent both Anglo and Hispanic settlers and ranchers from making more and more inroads into traditional Zuni territories that did not legally form part of the reservation. Toward the end of the nineteenth century, this encroachment became especially severe on the eastern and southern portions of Zuni land; in the western portion the Mormons were also expanding their holdings. As the population of immigrant communities grew, the Zuni lost access to most of their former territory, especially areas located near springs and streams, which were especially desirable to settlers. These new settlements prevented the Zuni from grazing their animals, hunting, and gathering wild plants in familiar places that they had used for centuries. Not surprisingly, the result was a number of conflicts over land use, some of them bloody.

American companies also began to exploit the natural resources in Zuni territory during the late 1800s. Timber companies started clear-cutting large portions of forest in the Zuni Mountains in the 1890s. In just over 10 years, more than 2 billion feet (610 million meters) of timber were cut—and once the trees were gone, white American cattle and sheep owners grazed their animals on the deforested land, eliminating any chance of reforestation.

Other Native American groups were also competing for Zuni land. Navajos and Apaches seeking refuge from U.S. Army troops and aggressive white American settlers entered Zuni territory in the mid- and late nineteenth century and resumed raiding Zuni farms and villages. In one especially serious incident in 1850, more than 100 Navajo held the village of Zuni under siege for 16 days. The Zuni later retaliated by killing 30 Navajo, and Zuni guides and spies assisted U.S. troops in their war against the Navajo (although Zuni traders were an important source of supplies for the Navajo and Apache tribes during their wars with the United States).

The conflicts between the Zuni, Navajo, and Apache reflected the crowding that all Native American groups were experiencing as American settlers, backed by U.S. troops, moved onto their lands. Both the Navajo and the Apache had been forced from their traditional territories, and it mattered little to U.S. authorities if the land available for them to live on had historically belonged to another tribe. Eventually, the Navajo settled in the northern areas of traditional Zuni territory, while the Apache settled in the southern and western sections. In 1868, the U.S. government established boundaries for a Navajo reservation that included a northern section of traditional Zuni territory, and three years later, some Apache settled on a reservation that took in a southwestern area of traditional Zuni lands. The establishment of such new reservations forced the Zuni to confine themselves more to their relatively small reservation area during a time when their population was finally beginning to increase after centuries of decline.

RELIGIOUS INTERFERENCE

The Zuni also faced increased efforts by missionaries and U.S. government officials to interfere with their traditional religious life. In 1897, Mary E. DeSette, the teacher at the Presbyterian day school, had several Bow Priests arrested for persecuting a witch. (She was entirely unaware of and probably equally unconcerned about the complex nature of the crime of witchcraft in Zuni society.) DeSette, who had previously distinguished herself by instigating a haircutting campaign (Zuni men wore long hair) and by threatening to cancel the Shalako festival, was a deeply disruptive force on the reservation, mainly because she felt that the Zuni would respect her and accept her authority only if she, as she put it in a letter to the U.S. commissioner of Indian affairs, "stir[red] up the authorities" at every possible occasion. In keeping with this philosophy, DeSette arranged for U.S. Army troops to aid the local sheriff in arresting the Bow Priests. Although the charges against the priests were dropped and the government released them after only a few months (and after having their hair cut off), the troops occupied

Zuni for nearly a year at DeSette's request. According to historian C. Gregory Crampton in *The Zunis of Cibola,* "Throughout the affair the Zunis remained calm, though they may well have had some misgivings about future trends in education." The presence of U.S. troops acting as law enforcement seriously undermined the authority of the Bow Priests; this erosion of authority was intensified because those priests who had had their hair cut off in prison were considered defiled and could no longer participate in important religious ceremonies.

Not surprisingly, the Presbyterian mission did not attract huge numbers of converts at this time, nor did the Christian (Dutch) Reformed Church, which established a mission at Zuni in 1897. As in past centuries, the Zuni's participation in traditional religious societies and rituals oriented their lives around common activities and shared meanings, and giving up such meaningful traditions did not come easily. In addition, the common demand that Christian converts give up any involvement in traditional Zuni religious practices was completely antithetical to many Zuni, who held that the different religious beliefs were not entirely incompatible. As one missionary lamented, "The most common reaction of Zunis to the gospel message is that the Jesus-way and the Zuni-way are 'hi-ni-na,' 'the same.'"

The U.S. government continued to interfere with Zuni political institutions. They ignored the traditional separation of religious leaders from direct secular political involvement by insisting that the Bow Priests select the secular leaders. Federal authorities instituted a tribal council consisting of a governor and a number of assistants who were chosen for office each year. The tribal council, though, was far from independent. Instead, any of its decisions could be implemented only if U.S. government officials approved.

ENGLISH-LANGUAGE EDUCATION

During the late nineteenth and early twentieth centuries, the U.S. government became more directly involved in regulating the education of Native Americans. The federal government had decided that attempts should be made to "civilize" Native Americans by having children attend schools where they could learn American customs and values. English-language instruction was viewed as critical to this effort; consequently, the use of Native languages was banned in schools. The U.S. commissioner of Indian affairs clearly enunciated reasons for this policy as far back as 1887, stating:

> Instruction of Indians in the vernacular is not only of no use to them but is detrimental to the cause of education and civilization and will not be permitted in any Indian school. This language which is good enough for a white person ought to be good enough for the red person. It is also believed that teaching Indians in their own barbarous dialect is a positive detriment to them. The impracticability, if not impossibility of civilizing Indians in any other tongue than our own would seem obvious.

After the DeSette affair of 1897, the U.S. government took closer control of the schools at Zuni, ending the subsidization of mission schools and opening a government day school instead. Besides the day school, the U.S. government opened a boarding school in 1907, and the Christian (Dutch) Reformed Church opened a nonsubsidized mission day school in 1908. These schools offered basic subjects, such as writing and reading, cooking and sewing for girls, and manual skills for boys. Such formal education became relatively popular early on, in part because there were now a number of schools on the reservation, so a student who had trouble adjusting at one school could always transfer to another one. The English-only policy of these schools was initially supported by the Zuni, who felt that their children would learn Zuni at home anyway and that knowledge of English would be a valuable skill when negotiating among Americans. In later years, however, the Zuni would pressure their schools into becoming more bilingual and placing more emphasis on Zuni culture.

CHANGES IN AGRICULTURE

The twentieth century saw yet another expansion of Zuni agriculture, as farmers adopted American technology, like plows, iron hoes, shovels, and rakes. Agricultural surpluses were sold for a profit to American traders and residents of nearby towns, such as Gallup, New Mexico, and Holbrook, Arizona. The Zuni also sold corn, wheat, and other farm products to soldiers at Fort Defiance and Fort Wingate. Federal efforts to increase farming on the Zuni Reservation were motivated by policies to encourage individual economic endeavors in Native communities throughout the country and to break up communal land ownership patterns. To further agricultural development, the government began construction of a large dam and reservoir in 1903 at a site called Black Rock on the Zuni River. Construction of the dam, however, took many years and encountered many problems. First, few Zuni agreed to work on the project, preferring instead to continue their traditional work as herders and small-scale farmers and their participation in seasonal religious rituals. Second, large amounts of silt from the soil became deposited in the reservoir, limiting its capacity and interfering with the flow and purity of the water that was supposed to eventually reach Zuni fields. And third, a decrease in federal funds led to the postponement of improvements. Despite these problems, by 1920 the reservoir contributed to an increase in Zuni acreage to 4,380 acres (1,772 hectares) from an earlier estimate of 500 to 600 acres (202 to 242 hectares). In the following year, though, further problems with the reservoir led to a steady decline in water supply so that by 1935 there was only enough water to irrigate 935 acres (378 hectares).

During this period, however, substantial increases in rainfall contributed to a boom in Zuni farming. In this context, a new farming settlement was established in 1912 called Tekapo (meaning "full of hills"), located southwest of Zuni on the Zuni River.

Zuni ranching also prospered in the early twentieth century. By 1910, Zuni ranchers owned approximately 65,000 head of sheep, more than double the number they had in 1880. The Zuni Reservation contained about 285,000 acres (115,335 hectares), and as the herds grew, the problem of finding adequate land to graze them on became critical. Zuni leaders and agents of the federal Bureau of

Indian Affairs (BIA) repeatedly asked the president and Congress to enlarge the reservation, but instead of adding to Zuni territory, Congress took land away from the reservation in 1910 to create national forests in the area. The Zuni protested, and two years later President William Taft reversed the decision, returning the land. Finally, in 1917, President Woodrow Wilson issued an executive order that added about 80,000 acres (32,374 hectares) to the Zuni Reservation. Additional acreage was included in 1935 and in 1940, bringing the total above 400,000 acres (161,874 hectares). In addition to traditional agricultural sources of income, some Zuni worked for railroads, government agencies, and businesses in nearby Anglo towns.

VILLAGE AND GOVERNMENT

Changes also took place in the village of Zuni itself. Although the basic design of the houses did not change, new homes were built with larger rooms and higher ceilings. Defensive concerns were no longer paramount, so ground-level doors and windows became common. In addition, many upper-story dwellings were taken down, and more ground-level homes were built. The Zuni no longer had to cluster all their buildings together for defensive purposes, so outlying houses, built at some distance from the main village, became more common, with 81 families (about 37 percent of the population) living in these "suburbs" by 1915.

The Zuni government also reflected both continuity and change as the twentieth century progressed. At the beginning of the century, the two governing councils—one consisting of religious leaders whose decisions were enforced by the Bow Priests and one entirely secular in nature, consisting of a governor, a lieutenant governor, and councillors—coexisted and shared power. But the authority of the Bow Priests, already threatened by the DeSette affair, was further undermined when the U.S. government decided to exercise closer control over the Zuni by opening a local BIA office near Zuni in 1902. The new agency was headed by an agent who supervised federal programs and local activities.

BIA agents also advised Zuni secular leaders and had authority to approve or veto decisions of the council.

In 1916, the BIA agent to the Zuni became involved in a controversy that deeply affected Zuni politics. That year, a group of Catholic clergy proposed building a new mission in Zuni. When a public meeting was called to discuss the request, all in attendance signaled their opposition by a voice vote. A small group of Zuni Roman Catholics, however, appealed to the BIA agent (himself a Roman Catholic), who donated a plot of village land for the construction of the church. The church, named St. Anthony's Mission Church, was completed in 1922, over the opposition of the majority of the Zuni. Those opposed to the mission became known as Protestants (although many were not practitioners of any Christian religion), while those who supported the mission became known as Catholics (whether or not they were actually Roman Catholic)—a political division that has continued to this day.

EFFECTS OF THE MERIAM REPORT

In 1928, a U.S. government study known as the Meriam Report revealed that many Native American tribes lived in abysmally poor conditions. These conditions would be improved, the report suggested, by increased federal funding to the tribes, as well as greater tribal control over how such funds were spent. Several years later, John Collier, who became the commissioner of Indian affairs in 1933, responded to these findings by urging Congress to pass new legislation to give tribal governing councils authority over development programs on their reservations. Although Collier was willing to hand over a considerable amount of power to the tribal councils, he also wanted to regulate their functioning and establish guidelines for the selection of councillors in a manner that was not always consistent with tribal traditions.

With Collier's urging, Congress passed legislation known as the Indian Reorganization Act (IRA) in 1934. The IRA provided that the reservations adopt formal constitutions and elect their

Before becoming commissioner, John Collier (*above*, with a group of Crow) openly criticized the Bureau of Indian Affairs for failing to enact legislation beneficial to Native Americans. He later urged Congress to grant Native American groups some authority over their own reservations.

tribal leaders. Each reservation had the option of accepting or rejecting the IRA's provisions through a local referendum. Andrew Trotter, the BIA superintendent in charge of the Zuni agency, was instrumental in persuading the Zuni—who at the time were in the midst of a bitter dispute between the Catholics and the Protestants that threatened to render the village ungovernable—to adopt the IRA provisions.

Once the IRA was accepted, Trotter appointed a committee of six members to nominate two candidates for governor. After the nominations were made, a public meeting was held at which all men in attendance could vote. The candidate who received the most votes became governor, while the losing candidate became lieutenant governor. Besides the gubernatorial election, six members of a tribal council were also selected, each representing a different district. Under the new regulations, all tribal leaders served terms of one year. The nominating committee appointed by Trotter functioned for two years, after which members of the committee were elected by male voters until 1965, when women obtained the franchise. Obviously, this new system of choosing leaders was extremely different from the traditional system, in which religious leaders appointed the members of the local government. According to C. Gregory Crampton, "The transition from a theocratic form of government to one based on popular consent was not achieved without much division and debate, anxiety, stress, tension, and soul-searching. People still take sides on the form of government the Zunis should have."

The 1930s witnessed other federal initiatives that also had long-term consequences for the Zuni. For the first time since the reservation was established in 1877, the U.S. government carried out an extensive survey of the boundaries of Zuni land. When the survey was completed in 1934, government workers erected a fence around the reservation's borders. Before this time, Zuni herders had routinely grazed their animals in adjacent pastures, but after the reservation was fenced in, they were restricted to the land within the reservation. This reduction in grazing area quickly resulted in a depletion of good forage and erosion of the soil. In response to the worsening situation, Collier instituted a program of stock reduction aimed at limiting the number of animals owned by Native Americans. The Zuni Reservation was divided into 18 grazing units, and each was given a quota of livestock based on what federal authorities thought the unit could sustain. If herders in the unit had holdings that exceeded the limit, they were forced to sell the surplus animals to the U.S. government at fixed prices.

The Zuni vigorously protested the stock-reduction program. Zuni herders were never consulted during the development of the

Federal officials fenced in the Zuni reservation after a land survey in 1934. Because the Zuni relied heavily on herding, many families saw a decrease in their source of income.

program, and they resented what they saw as high-handed interference with their livelihood. Many families had to give up a large portion of their herds, thereby losing a stable source of income. The prices the U.S. government paid herders for their sheep were low, and a onetime payment for herds did not reflect the sheep's true value, because herders sold wool from the same animals year after year. Despite these losses, Zuni herders made a slow economic recovery after World War II.

FIGHTING FOR THEIR COUNTRY

The 1940s also saw more than 200 Zuni men leave the village to fight for the United States in World War II. Many of these men were volunteers, and others were drafted into the army. Some cases stirred controversy, though. For example, a Zuni Rain Priest applied for and was granted a religious deferral based on his role as a religious practitioner. As quoted in Paul Rosier's *Serving Their Country*, the Zuni had argued that his services were "needed to bring rain not only for the [Zuni Reservation] but for the whole world."

Many Zuni soldiers were exposed to new countries and new cultures, and some came back expounding ideas and exhibiting behavior that their elders found distinctly non-Zuni, which resulted for a short while in a good deal of generational friction. The veterans quickly reintegrated themselves into Zuni life, however, participating in dances and religious ceremonies and using their G.I. benefits to obtain vocational and agricultural training. But often when they returned from the war, they became acutely aware of the legal limitations they faced because of discriminatory government policies. For example, in his autobiography, Zuni war veteran Virgil Wyaco remarked that ". . . even though I'd risked my life fighting overseas, I could neither vote nor drink alcohol in New Mexico under state law because I was an Indian." He added, "When they drafted me, I was expected to serve like everybody else, but I couldn't vote because I was an Indian. When I got out, I couldn't have a beer with my friends in college because it was against the law to serve Indians liquor."

By the mid-twentieth century, the Zuni had adjusted to changed conditions brought about by pressures from outside forces, incorporating new technologies and activities into their lives while keeping faith in their own values and beliefs.

TERMINATION

In the 1950s, the U.S. government drew up plans for a new policy toward Native American reservations. This policy sought to terminate the special obligations that the federal government had toward Indian reservations and to end the special legal status of the reservations themselves. To begin, a number of reservations in California, the Upper Midwest, and the Northwest were chosen for "Termination." Most Native American communities strenuously opposed this new policy because they believed that the U.S. government had enduring obligations to protect the Native reservations stemming from treaties signed in the eighteenth and nineteenth centuries. Although the Zuni were not directly targeted for Termination, their representatives contributed their voices in opposition. For example, Zuni veterans of World War II and the Korean War sent a written statement to Congress, quoted in Paul Rosier's *Serving Their Country,* in which they said that many Native Americans had "fought for democracy" in the wars. The statement went on to say:

> We would like to have you show us this democratic way of life. We have served [overseas] in order to save our country, our people, our religion, our freedom of the press, and our freedom of speech from destruction. . . . We, now in the land of freedom as Americans, are faced with [Termination policies] which will mean total destruction of all tribes.

Although the Zuni were spared this direct threat, their communities have continued to face pressures to alter their traditional ways of life. They have continued to meet these pressures, as they have since the sixteenth century, with the same remarkable ability to incorporate new elements while retaining their own distinctive identities.

Contemporary Issues

Many changes have taken place in the Zuni's lives in recent years. The reservation, consisting of 418,304 acres (169,281 hectares), or more than 700 square miles (1,800 square kilometers) of land, was home to 5,973 people (3,100 women and 2,873 men) in 2007—a dramatic recovery from the low of 1,514 people recorded in 1905. Census data also indicate the continued strength of Zuni families: In 2007, 89.7 percent of the Zuni lived in family-based households, while only 10.3 percent lived alone or with non-family members. These numbers differ from those of New Mexico as a whole, where the percentage of family-based households was a reported 68.8 percent. Indeed, the ratio of Zuni households based on family membership was the highest among all U.S. population groups.

The reservation itself has undergone modernization in terms of housing, public services, and transportation. In the 1950s, improvements were made in public services that included the installation of electricity, the construction of a piped water system, the paving of roads, and the completion of a sewer system and indoor plumbing.

The community of Zuni now contains two distinct types of housing. In the old central section of town, the houses primarily retain the traditional Zuni designs, although they have been modernized and enlarged. New homes—mostly single-family dwellings, some with small lawns—have been constructed in suburban areas outside Zuni. These homes are of various styles, some with gabled or pitched roofs and some built from wood, cinder block, and other materials. The location of traditional kivas and open plazas has remained the same, but new public facilities have been added to Zuni, including a large building that contains the headquarters of the tribal council and other government offices. The community at Black Rock, the site of the Bureau of Indian Affairs agency, located several miles to the northeast of Zuni, has also increased in size. An airstrip was built there in 1967, and the community is the home of a hospital run by the U.S. Public Health Service.

A DIVERSE ECONOMY

The Zuni economy has grown and diversified since the middle of the twentieth century. Sources of income include farming, herding, wage work, and craft production. Farming continues to be an important endeavor, although most rely on farming only for supplemental income. Only about 1,000 acres (404 hectares) of Zuni land are under cultivation, a sharp decrease from the 10,000 to 12,000 acres (4,046 to 4,856 hectares) farmed in the nineteenth century. Major crops today include corn, pinto beans, wheat, chili, cabbage, onions, and beets, which are either consumed in the household or sold to nearby markets. As in past centuries, men do most of the farming, although a number of older women still plant small traditional waffle gardens near their homes.

The Zuni have expanded and upgraded water supplies to increase farm production and livestock holdings, digging numerous wells throughout the reservation and developing the natural springs at Nutria, Pescado, and Ojo Caliente. Approximately 95 percent of the reservation's land is now used for grazing. The reservation is divided into 95 grazing units for sheepherding, each assigned to a specific herder or group of herders. Four pastures for cattle are assigned to two cattle associations.

All use of grazing land is regulated by provisions of the Zuni Range Code, adopted in 1976. The code issues permits to herders and sets limits on the number of animals allowed in each grazing unit or cattle range. If owners exceed their annual quotas, they must sell the surplus. The Zuni A:shiwi Livestock Committee was formed in 1992 to supervise the use of rangelands. It updates and enforces the range code, recommends range improvements, and resolves any conflicts that arise over land use. Improvements have been made in rangelands through tribal programs that reseed the land, remove unwanted trees, and restore pasture.

The Zuni are developing additional uses of their land to provide tribal and individual income. Public and private concerns mine deposits of sand, gravel, and limestone for the construction and paving of roads on and near the reservation. At one time, the Bureau of Indian Affairs operated four mines to exploit the substantial coal deposits near Nutria and Pescado. These mines are now defunct but may reopen in the future, as may the historic copper mines in the Zuni Mountains. The Zuni have also stocked their reservoirs with fish for recreational purposes.

ZUNI ARTISANS

Many Zuni are self-employed as silversmiths or artisans. Silversmithing began in Zuni communities in the late nineteenth century. The first Zuni silversmith, a man named Lanyade, learned to fashion silver into jewelry from a well-known Navajo artisan named Atsidi Chon in 1872. Lanyade taught silverwork to a number of Zuni men, who then set up a workshop where they shared tools and raw materials. Soon, the price of tools and materials declined so that silversmiths did not need to work communally

Zuni artisans have become famous for silversmithing, a long tradition within the tribe. Often decorated with turquoise and religious motifs, Zuni silver jewelry has become popular throughout the world.

but instead could produce in their own homes. At first, the craft was restricted to men, continuing the traditional gender roles that assigned metalwork as a male occupation. By the late 1920s, women began to participate in silversmithing, learning from and helping their husbands. Women may now work independently, although in many cases, husbands and wives form a team, allocating separate tasks in the process of jewelry making to each spouse.

Zuni silversmiths produce jewelry in two distinctive styles, needlepoint and inlay. In the needlepoint style, small bits of turquoise are cut and mounted in silver to form patterns on rings, necklaces, bracelets, and pins. In the inlay technique, small pieces of shell, coral, jet, and turquoise are cut into different shapes and mounted in a base of silver. Silversmiths sell their jewelry to retailers in Gallup, Santa Fe, Albuquerque, and many other cities in the United States, Canada, Europe, and Asia. Two organizations, the Zuni Craftsmen's Cooperative Association and the Zuni Arts and Crafts Enterprise, market jewelry to local and national outlets and promote silversmiths, potters, painters, and sculptors.

Pottery making was once an important activity, engaged in by most Zuni women to provide household ware for their families. By the early twentieth century, however, pottery making had declined because of the time-consuming nature of the process and the availability of cheaper, store-bought vessels. Now, since the 1970s, the art of ceramics has been revived in Zuni communities by women and men, although women potters still predominate. Indeed, ceramics classes are taught in Zuni middle and high schools, with many students producing work individually and communally.

Jewelry and pottery making are usually part-time specialties that people pursue to supplement their incomes from other work. But some Zuni have become full-time artists in these fields, especially in silversmithing. Their work is innovative and original, in terms of design and materials, while keeping within traditional Zuni motifs. Their pieces are purchased by museums and collectors of fine art. In a discussion of his work, included in *Zuni: A*

Village of Silversmiths, Charles Hustito commented on the styles that are distinctively Zuni:

> You see a certain piece of work and you can identify the origins of where that pattern came from even though it is the great-grandchildren who are doing it. It is carried on from generation to generation. Selection of colors has not that much to do with identity—it is the pattern and design and nature of the silverwork that distinguishes families. I appreciate the fact that people are taking pride in their work. And that is how I believe each Zuni craftsman feels about their work. I believe the Zuni people want to maintain their identity through the crafts that they started off with.

Some Zuni artists produce objects called *Ahayu:da* that have great religious significance. Ahayu:da are representative images of the Twin Gods (sometimes referred to as the War Gods), who are the Zuni's protectors. The images are made of wood and decorated with paint and feathers. They are placed in outdoor shrines surrounding the Zuni pueblo until they deteriorate naturally and return to the earth in a normal cycle of decay. In the Zuni view, "all things will eat themselves up." The Zuni believe that whenever Ahayu:da are taken from their shrines, disaster may ensue.

Zuni artists have been making sacred images for centuries, but many older works were bought or stolen from the Zuni by visitors and were eventually acquired by museums and private galleries and collectors. In 1978, the Zuni began to seek the return of their Ahayu:da, and by 1995, 80 such objects had been returned in 46 separate transfers by museums such as the Smithsonian Institution in Washington, D.C., the National Museum of the American Indian in New York City, and the Museum of New Mexico. Private galleries and individual collectors have also returned several carvings.

In attempting to secure the return of the Ahayu:da, the Zuni Tribal Council was acting in conjunction with Zuni religious

As with many other tribes and nations, explorers and tourists have stolen or bought valuable Zuni artifacts. These items have enormous religious and cultural value, and many are in the process of being returned to their owners. Above, this feathered headdress belongs to tribes outside of New Mexico but was found in Santa Fe.

leaders, who held a series of meetings and issued a declaration in September 1978. The statement read in part:

> All religious items/artifacts/objects, no matter how insignificant it/they may seem to non-Zunis, are of very high/great religious value. They are in fact, the essence of our Zuni culture. . . . The majority of these items were created by groups of religious orders, each having skill or expertise in a specific aspect of the Zuni religious culture. The majority of these items have been created for the benefit of all the Zuni people, and are communally owned. . . . No one individual or group of individuals has the right to remove communally owned religious items from the Zuni land for any purpose whatsoever. . . . The theft and removal of sacred items has created an imbalance in the spiritual world. In order to restore harmony to all living things, this balance needs to be restored. . . . This decision [to request the return of sacred items] is based on our desires to perpetuate our Zuni culture in its full/total context with the blessing of our spiritual fathers, mothers, and children which are rightfully ours.

Another result of the Zuni's efforts to repossess their Ahayu:da was the passage in Congress of the Native American Graves Protection and Repatriation Act of 1990, which provides for the return of Native American artifacts and grave remains to the tribe from which they were taken. The Zuni were instrumental in achieving passage of this important legislation. Since then, the tribe has repatriated additional objects of cultural significance. The Zuni have not, however, sought the return of human remains taken from archaeological excavations and kept in museums because they believe that the bodies have been irreparably desecrated by removal from their graves and that no remedy can reverse the harm. Instead, the Zuni request that the remains be cared for respectfully. The Zuni Tribal Council has enacted its own regulations regarding the excavation of burials. It insists that no graves be disturbed except as necessary for development projects.

In these cases, the human remains uncovered must be reburied as quickly as possible and as close to their original site as possible.

GOVERNMENT STRUCTURE

The political structure of the tribe underwent a good deal of change during the 1970s. In 1970, the Zuni adopted a formal constitution, and the U.S. government recognized the Zuni Tribal Council as the official legislative body, with the right to control the local government and organize elections. In 1974, the Zuni eliminated the nominating committee and instituted popular elections, in which candidates run on their own behalf. The governor, lieutenant governor, and members of the tribal council are now elected to four-year terms.

Soon after taking office, in 1974, the Tribal Council voted to establish a reservation-based school district so that Zuni parents could have more control over their children's education. Until that time, Zuni children were part of a local New Mexico school district, whose board was dominated by Anglo parents and their interests. Five schools now serve the reservation.

Another educational issue concerned the continuation of a school called the Southwestern Indian Polytechnic Institute (or SIPI) in Albuquerque. The Zuni and the other southwestern Native nations had organized SIPI in 1970 as a technical school to serve their populations. The school was located not far from the reservations and had dormitories to house Native students. In 1982, though, James Watts, the secretary of the interior, threatened to close it. The SIPI board, under Zuni director Virgil Wyaco, lobbied congressional representatives and also filed a lawsuit against the threatened closure. They argued that SIPI had been established under provisions of the Indian Education Act and the Indian Reorganization Act and that closing it without an act of Congress was illegal. In testimony before a Senate committee, Wyaco told the senators that "SIPI is a different kind of school, designed for young, full-time students but with enough flexibility that time could be taken for required home visits without penalty," thereby allowing students to participate in community and family rituals and other obligations. Finally, Watts was forced to reverse his order.

LAND RIGHTS

One area of critical concern for the tribal council, and for all Zuni, is land rights and compensation for land taken illegally during the past centuries. The Zuni lobbied for the return of Zuni Salt Lake, which not only provides salt but is also an important religious site. In 1978, the U.S. Congress enacted legislation directing the federal government to acquire Zuni Salt Lake from the State of New Mexico and return it to the tribe. The late Robert Lewis, who served as governor of Zuni Pueblo on and off for nearly three decades, was among those officials who helped return Zuni Salt Lake to its rightful owners.

A dispute over another sacred area ended in victory for the Zuni in the 1980s. The tribe filed a suit for the return of a site called Koluwala-wa, located at the juncture of the Zuni and Little Colorado rivers. Koluwala-wa is the focus of pilgrimages made every four years by religious leaders who ask the deities there for rain to nurture the land and crops, and it is one of the places where Zuni souls go after death. In 1984, the Zuni won the return of Koluwala-wa, but ranchers who owned surrounding land sometimes denied them access to the area. After years of protest in court, the Zuni were granted the permanent right to cross private land on their ritual journeys to Koluwala-wa.

In addition to suits for the return of land, the Zuni submitted a claim to the U.S. Court of Indian Claims in 1978 for monetary compensation for land taken from them in the nineteenth and twentieth centuries. The Court of Claims issued a ruling in 1987 giving the Zuni title to a large portion of present-day Arizona and New Mexico and stating that the tribe had been wrongfully deprived of 14,835,892 acres (6,003,872 hectares) of their land during the period from 1876 to 1939. Following years of negotiation, the Zuni were awarded $25 million as compensation for their land. The award was deposited in a trust fund and is awaiting the tribe's decision on how to put it to best use.

In 1990, the Zuni reached an agreement with the U.S. government that ended another legal suit. In the 1970s, they had sued the U.S. government for neglecting its responsibilities to protect Zuni land, as pledged in the treaties signed between the two nations. The tribe claimed that the U.S. government had illegally sold Zuni land to a number of non-Zuni, including railroad companies that were extending track through the Southwest at the turn of the twentieth century and U.S. officers stationed at Fort Wingate who wished to open private ranches. In addition, the U.S. government permitted ranchers to encroach on and to overgraze Zuni land, and it allowed timber companies to overcut Zuni forests. Finally, the U.S. government permitted the mining of coal and salt from Zuni territory without compensating the tribe.

ZUNI CONSERVATION PROJECT

The suit against the United States ended in an agreement ratified by Congress as the Zuni Land Conservation Act of 1990, which established a permanent, $25 million Zuni Indian Resource Development Trust Fund. Interest from the fund is used to create and implement the Zuni Sustainable Resource Development Plan, aimed at developing renewable resources on the reservation, rehabilitating the reservation's watershed and water resources, and acquiring land for future use. The plan is overseen and implemented by the Zuni Conservation Project, directed by James Enote, which aims to replant vegetation, control soil erosion, improve soil quality, and reduce the loss of water. The Conservation Project collects data on fish and wildlife resources, water sources, and forestry needs, and it began a program at Nutria in 1992 to gather data on local conditions, including the quality of soil, water resources, crop needs, and labor skills of Zuni farmers. A list of the projects implemented or considered gives an overview of the kinds of issues that the Zuni think are important for the maintenance and development of their territory and their culture.

Watershed Restoration

These projects are aimed at repairing land and restoring the Zuni watershed. Particularly in the arid Southwest, watershed restoration depends on land management policies. For the Zuni, land management focuses on farming and grazing livestock, especially sheep and cattle. Some of the projects included watershed treatments; tribal forest treatments; repairs to erosion-control structures; peach orchard rehabilitation; protection and development of natural springs; and fish and wildlife wetland and meadow development.

Hydrology

The water resources in Zuni territory are relatively limited; year-round flowing rivers are lacking, although there are a number of small springs. Additional water for irrigating crops and replenishing the soil comes from rain and groundwater. The Zuni tribe recognizes that its growing population puts additional strain on resources. Therefore, water sources need to be protected in quality and developed in quantity. Hydrology projects included coordination of an early warning flood system; rangeland water development designs; assistance to the Zuni Solid Waste Program; technical support to the Zuni Water Rights Program; and assistance in sewage treatment and artificial wetland planning.

Geographic Information Systems

The Zuni tribe developed a computerized system to help manage resources, collect data, and coordinate programs concerning irrigation, agricultural fields, and grazing lands. It mapped the growth of crops, grazing units, and water resources.

Range Conservation

Concerned with managing rangeland, the Zuni recognize that most available grazing lands are located in arid or semi-arid areas with sparse grass and shrubs, factors conducive to high levels of erosion. Conservation projects included range water development; annual vegetation surveys; windmill repair; and review of range carrying capacity data and policy.

Sustainable Agriculture

Today, only a small number of Zuni are continuing their tradition of farming. Most Zuni farmers grow vegetables, alfalfa, and other forage crops in small gardens near their houses. The tribe, however, has responded to renewed interest in farming by developing projects aimed at sustainable agriculture. Such projects included assistance to the Zuni Organic Farmers Cooperative; discovery and rehabilitation of old peach orchards; developing gardens at community schools; maintaining the Zuni Community Seedbank; maintaining the community compost project; and completion of annual crop surveys.

Community Forests

The Zuni tribe is interested in developing forest resources principally for local use. Projects emphasized the importance of maintaining and expanding forest ecology, especially stands of piñon and juniper, the only types of trees that grow in abundance in Zuni territory.

MAINTAINING CULTURAL HERITAGE

Other tribal projects seek to preserve the Zuni's cultural heritage and advance the tribe's opportunities for the future. The A:shiwi A:wan Museum and Heritage Center (*A:shiwi A:wan* means "belonging to the Zuni people") was founded to maintain, display, and enhance knowledge of Zuni history and culture. In the words of the museum's statement of purpose, it is not a "temple" for the past, but "a community learning center which links the past with the present as a strategy to deal with the future." The museum has an archive that keeps documents of all tribal activities, and

Many young Zuni keep their culture alive by participating in community dances and cultural events. Above, young women perform the traditional Zuni deer dance.

it publishes a quarterly newsletter containing information about programs at the museum and elsewhere in the community. News about local events and current issues is also relayed on the Zuni radio station, KSHI-FM, founded in 1977.

The Zuni proudly maintain many aspects of their traditional culture. Families are bound together with strong feelings of communal loyalty and support, and matrilineal clans continue to determine an individual's social and group identity. The Zuni language is still the first language of most people. The entire community unites to celebrate sacred rituals that have as much meaning for modern Zuni as they did for their ancestors. In the words of a Zuni storyteller:

> Today as we live in the present ways of our people, we live also within the realm of our ancestors, for we are sustained through the rituals and beliefs of long ago. We live in accordance to the ways of our people, which bring life, blessings, and happiness.

The Zuni in the Twenty-First Century

As the Zuni prosper in the twenty-first century, they can feel secure in a number of significant successes in their struggle to maintain their land and their rights of access to sacred places. Although their economy is improving, however, the Zuni still suffer from some of the same economic hardships as most other Native Americans, especially those living on reservations.

LAND RIGHTS BATTLES CONTINUE

Despite the return of Zuni Salt Lake in 1978, the tribe's efforts to preserve that sacred location were still not over. In August 2003, the Zuni won a major victory in their fight to protect the lake, which is believed to be the home of Salt Woman (also called Salt Mother), one of their most revered deities. For centuries the lake, located 60 miles (97 kilometers) southeast of the Zuni Reservation, has been the destination of pilgrimages by the Zuni as well as members of other Southwestern indigenous nations. Pilgrims have gone there to seek spiritual advice and make offerings to the deities to show them honor and respect. Zuni Rain Priests go to the lake on annual pilgrimages to pray for the rain so necessary in the arid Southwest. People also collect salt from the rich saline water for use in ceremonies as well as for everyday domestic purposes. According to Zuni tradition, the land surrounding the lake has been an area of sanctuary and peace.

In the late 1980s, though, a private utility power company based in Arizona, called Salt River Project (SRP), began to buy land around the Salt Lake. Its plan was to develop an 18,000-acre (7,284-hectare) strip mine for coal, only 10 miles (16 kilometers) from the lake. The plan included the use of up to 85 gallons (322 liters) of water every minute for a period of 40 years to process the coal. Finally, the plan included a 44-mile (71-kilometer) railroad line that would extend from the mine to a generating station. The rail line would cut across burial grounds and sacred pilgrimage routes. Even in the preliminary stages, the company destroyed Zuni property. During initial survey work, SRP crews unearthed seven bodies of Zuni ancestors that needed to be reburied according to Zuni custom.

The Zuni immediately began to protest the plan, citing the sacred value of the lake and its surrounding territory. They also feared that the company's use of water would have a disastrous effect on the delicate desert aquifers that feed the lake. The people forged coalitions with other Native groups and with environmental organizations, such as the Sierra Club, urging intervention by the federal government. In 2001, the Zuni and their allies formed the Zuni Salt Lake Coalition to organize campaigns against SRP's plan. They sponsored a relay run from the Zuni Pueblo to Phoenix, Arizona, a distance of 700 miles (1,125 kilometers) round-trip to publicize their cause. Then, in July 2003, they held a People's Hearing at the Zuni Pueblo to discuss the situation. At the end of the hearing, attended by more than 500 people, a torrential thunderstorm suddenly appeared, unleashing heavy rains. Since rain has always been understood to be an omen from the spirit world, the Zuni interpreted the storm as a sign of spiritual support for their cause.

One month later, in August 2003, SRP management canceled its plans for the strip mine. The company stated that it would obtain cheaper, cleaner coal in Wyoming, but the pressure and publicity surrounding the Zuni sites must also have had an impact. In the words of Zuni Pueblo councilman Carlton Albert: "It has been a long 20-year struggle with a lot of mental anguish and frustration for our people, but we have had our voices heard. There is no word to express our appreciation to those who have given us help. If there is a lesson to be learned, it is to never give up and stay focused on what you want to accomplish." Carmelita Sanchez, the Zuni lieutenant governor, said: "It seemed like a burden was lifted from my heart and shoulders." Andy Bessler, an environmental activist working with the Sierra Club, stressed that the news was a "testament to the spirit of the Zuni people, other Native American tribes, and non-Native supporters who would not relinquish Salt Woman in the name of cheap coal." Finally, Governor Bill Richardson of New Mexico stated: "I think it's important to protect Native American religious sites." Zuni councilman Dan Simplicio concurred: "It's been a tremendous and costly battle, and I'm glad it's over. The awakening we had for the past two years was really strong. It awakened our powers of spiritual belief."

The Zuni's effort to protect the Salt Lake is just one of many battles fought by Native American groups to honor and maintain lands that they hold sacred. Some of these lands are believed to be places of origin of the people's ancestors. Others are thought to be inhabited by spirit beings or contain shrines where offerings are made to the deities. In a case related to the issue of sacred sites, the Zuni tribe, along with the nearby Hopi tribe and the Navajo Nation, won a victory in the U.S. Court of Appeals for the Ninth Circuit in 2004 when the judges issued a ruling that confirmed

In 2003, Zuni officials successfully stopped a private utility company from exploiting the natural resources around Zuni Salt Lake *(above)*. The plans to establish railroad tracks and a mine near the lake would have disturbed sacred Zuni burial grounds and pilgrimage routes.

the actions of Arizona's Department of Transportation, which had denied permits to a company seeking to exploit resources at Woodruff Butte, a sacred site. The company, Cholla Ready Mix, had sought to sell material mined at the butte for use in building and maintaining roads.

The court's decision recognized the "religious, cultural, and historical significance" of the region to the tribes. The judges based their decision, in part, on the fact that Woodruff Butte is eligible for listing in the National Register of Historic Places. Although the company had argued that, by protecting the site, Arizona was violating the U.S. Constitution's separation of church and state, the judges declared that Arizona was not promoting religion or any particular religion but instead was acting with a "secular purpose" by making sure that state construction projects do not "harm a site of religious, historical, and cultural importance to several Native American groups and the nation as a whole." Furthermore, "because of the unique status of Native American societies in North American history, protecting Native American shrines and other culturally important sites has historical value for the nation as a whole."

While this ruling applied particularly to Woodruff Butte, it has wider significance because it gives precedence to Native American concerns for their land over those of competing interests when specific cultural meanings can be demonstrated.

PROPOSED PROTECTIONS

Protection of sacred sites is the focus of legislation first introduced in Congress in 2003. The proposed law, called the Native American Sacred Lands Act, contains a number of significant features. It protects sacred sites on federally controlled land from development. To gain these protections, a Native American tribe would be required to supply evidence that the site has been used as part of traditional rituals or cultural practices and that its development would result in significant damage. Of particular importance is the fact that supporting evidence could be in the form of oral history or "Native science." According to the bill, "Native science"

> means the oral knowledge of Native Americans gained throughout history by observation and experience; embodies traditional lifestyles and values; is based on the fundamental belief in the sanctity of all life; is guided by principles that include interdependency, reciprocity, and the significance of place; is a living, spiritual knowledge of the relationships between the land, natural resources, and the environment; and is transferred from one generation to the next often through oral tradition and practice.

Recognition of the validity of oral history is an important advance in the protection of Native lands and cultures. It equates

Native Americans' knowledge and traditions with scientific or historical documents.

The Native American Sacred Lands Act has been introduced in several sessions of Congress but as of 2010 it had yet to be acted upon by the full body. Still, some courts and U.S. government agencies have respected the rights of Native Americans to their sacred sites by banning developments and sporting activities in their vicinity.

Besides their concerns about protecting sacred sites, the Zuni seek guarantees of respect for cultural resources and cultural knowledge. In testimony before the U.S. Senate Committee on Indian Affairs in 2002, then Zuni governor Malcolm Bowekaty stressed his people's desire to protect their sacred objects in the places where they are found. Although U.S. government regulations guarantee that objects will not be destroyed when construction or development occurs, the Zuni believe that part of the sacredness of such objects is related to the place where they are located. That is, since the ancestors and the deities have situated the objects in their specific locations, disturbing them or transporting them elsewhere violates their sanctity.

The Zuni also want to ensure the privacy of knowledge about ritual and spiritual matters. According to Bowekaty's testimony before Congress:

> The Zuni tribe finds itself in a bind when it comes to the release of esoteric information. While the federal agencies are very sensitive to our need to protect esoteric information, it is difficult for us to convey the importance of specific cultural resources without giving away information that is esoteric. [For instance] we attempt to explain that a plant is sacred to us without stating why it is sacred to us.

The Zuni continue to be in the forefront of the struggle for recognition of sacred sites. In 2010, Zuni governor Norman Cooeyate spoke before a meeting sponsored by the United Nations to

Universal Periodic Review

On March 16, 2010, Zuni governor Norman Cooeyate testified at a "Listening Session" to discuss the human rights record of the United States with Native Americans in preparation for the United Nations' "Universal Periodic Review." The review is conducted every four years under the guidelines of the Human Rights Council, which the United Nations General Assembly created in 2006 to evaluate member countries' compliance with human rights initiatives.

As cited in *A:shiwi News,* Governor Cooeyate stated:

As indigenous nations we are the children of the ancients who first walked on the lands which are the subject of my testimony. . . . Our songs, stories, religious practices, and our ancient gatherings together in this place of peace and refuge are part of us. The shrines, sacred paintings, places of prayer, and religious practices are near its springs, caves, canyons, and cliffs. The sacred plants, medicines and paints and animal places nurtured by this place are there. These are the essential and irreplaceable elements of the religious and cultural practices of our people.

We understand that everything in the natural world is alive and has power. . . . We recognize that each of these

review the human rights record of member countries. Cooeyate was chosen to represent the All Indian Pueblo Council and the Inter Tribal Council of Arizona on the topic of the United States' dealings with Native peoples seeking protection of sacred sites. Cooeyate reviewed negotiations between the Zuni and the federal government and concluded that Native tribes had been successful in gaining some of their rights but had met resistance and a lack of understanding of their claims from federal authorities.

elements works in concert with the other elements that make up an ecosystem. . . . All of these powers are influenced by the particular power of the place where they are found, so that the power of each ecosystem cannot be duplicated or replaced.

Our traditionalists use song cycles and ceremonies to and from this place . . . for the healing, protection, and physical and spiritual well-being and happiness of our tribes. . . . It has been a struggle to make the U.S. federal governmental agencies understand our reasons for requesting and seeking protection for such sites. All too often, we are requested to divulge all information related to the sites, to provide specific locations for such sites, and consider moving such sites as a way of mitigation. We are careful and discreet in the practices of our traditions, culture, and religion. We are hesitant to provide this information because it may not be received with the proper respect. All federal agencies need to understand that any desecration and destruction of sacred sites is like ripping a page out of a priceless novel. The stolen pages can never be replaced, repaired, nor will future readers be able to know the intended outcome.

We want the United States to uphold our right to protect our sacred places of prayer.

In keeping with their efforts to protect their land and all of its creatures, the Zuni have established an eagle aviary that cares for bald eagles and golden eagles that have been injured. These birds are treated and healed but remain unable to fend for themselves in the wild because of permanent foot or wing injuries. Besides caring for the birds, the Zuni collect the feathers that naturally drop from the eagles every day in the process of molting. These feathers are used in religious ceremonies and are sometimes sent to other tribes as well. The aviary has become a model for other tribes to follow.

TREASURES RETURN

One cultural resource recently returned to the Zuni is a collection of pottery taken between 1917 and 1924 by an archaeological expedition investigating the ancient trading center of Hawikuh. This was a center at an important crossroads where Native peoples from the Southwest came to exchange their goods. Some 20,000 artifacts were taken out of Hawikuh during the excavation for study and storage at the Smithsonian Institution in Washington, D.C. The Zuni have long considered these artifacts to be significant cultural resources documenting their prosperous history and the critical role they played in southwestern trade. In 2002, 75 pieces of pottery, representing the stylistic achievements of Zuni artisans, were returned to the Zuni Pueblo and displayed at an exhibition at the A:shiwi A:wan Museum and Heritage Center. Prior to the transfer of pots from the Smithsonian, Eileen Yatsattie, a contemporary Zuni potter, traveled to Washington, D.C., to advise the museum's staff on the cleaning and care of the pots.

Some Zuni have become cultural ambassadors to other countries. For example, a group of traditional Zuni dancers traveled to Mongolia in 2004 to participate in a program of indigenous music and dance. And Zuni artisans continue to participate in local and regional festivals that bring together the makers of pottery, basketry, jewelry, and other indigenous crafts for exhibition and sale.

The Zuni were at the forefront in calling for federal legislation to protect authentic Native American craftspeople. The tribe, along with its Hopi and Navajo neighbors, formed the Council for Indigenous Arts and Culture, based at the Zuni Reservation, to protect their cultural, artistic, and commercial interests. As a result of pressure from Native groups, the U.S. Congress passed the Indian Arts and Crafts Act in 1990, making it illegal to sell any art or craft product "in a manner that falsely suggests it is Indian

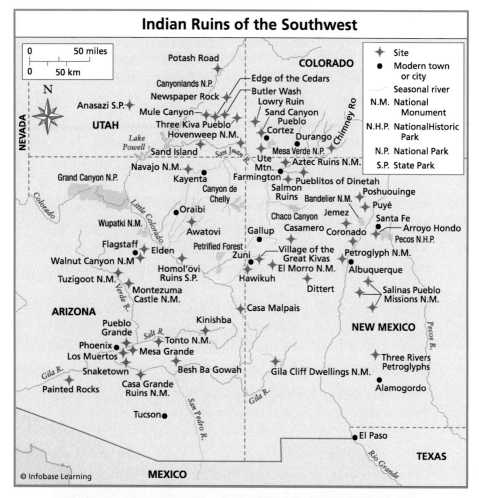

Indian Ruins of the Southwest

The Four Corners region of the Southwest is filled with ancient Native American ruins. Previous archaeological projects have excavated many religious and cultural relics from these sites, items the Zuni and other Native American groups are trying to recover.

produced, an Indian product, or the product of a particular Indian or Indian tribe or Indian arts and crafts organization." The act is aimed at protecting Native American artisans and the authenticity of their work. The legislation was in response to the proliferation of jewelry falsely labeled as authentic Indian. Much of the fake jewelry is produced abroad, by workers receiving low wages and using inferior materials. When these items are sold in the United States at low prices, they undercut the value of authentic works, which naturally cost more because of the skill of Native artisans and the high quality of their materials.

WATER RIGHTS

In consultation on another critical issue, the Zuni signed an agreement in 2004 with Gale Norton, the secretary of the Department of the Interior, that settled a controversy about water rights. The agreement concerned water levels in "Zuni Heaven," a sacred land that the tribe believes is the place of connection between the everyday world of the living and the spirit world of the dead and the deities. The area, once filled with "waist deep, swift moving streams," according to Zuni elders, is now virtually dry primarily to the construction of dams upstream that have diverted water. According to the agreement, the Zuni can have access to up to 3,600 acre-feet (4.4 million cubic meters) of water and up to 1,500 acre-feet (1.8 million cubic feet) from wells. This will help them in their attempts to return the area to its former wetlands condition. According to Wilford Eriacho, chair of the Zuni water rights negotiating team, "They are the most important lands from time immemorial. The water rights settlement will start to ease the hearts and minds of the Zuni people." Norton, the interior secretary, said: "It's important to protect and restore a sacred area. We need to have traditions that are long-standing and for our cultures to remain vibrant. Today's event has great significance for the cultural and natural future of the Southwest."

The settlement came with a price tag of $19.2 million paid by the federal government, while the State of Arizona contributed $1.6 million. With the money, the Zuni will establish a Zuni Indian Tribe Water Rights Development Fund to restore the land and purchase additional water rights.

In addition to securing water rights for sacred lands, the Zuni are moving forward with programs to develop sustainable agriculture projects on their reservation. For example, they are using traditional techniques such as "brush and rock structures" that keep back the rushing waters that occur when torrential summer rains hit the dry land. Although Zuni farming is dependent on rainfall, too much sudden water can destroy their crops. The structures, made by piling flat heavy rocks on top of juniper and sagebrush placed at the bottom of a gully, also retard soil erosion and retain water needed to irrigate the fields. These traditional methods of conserving water and protecting fields work as well, and sometimes better, than modern structures. Of course, they cost less.

Although the Zuni are proud of their age-old knowledge, they also adopt new technologies, using computers and sophisticated mapping techniques to record soil and weather conditions and monitor crop production. Among the main goals are protection of the Zuni watershed, rehabilitating traditional peach orchards, and developing wetlands as habitats for fish and wildlife. Monitoring and conserving rangeland and grazing territories for sheep, goats, and cattle are additional important tasks. Finally, protecting forest resources will help ensure their continuation for future generations.

EMPLOYMENT

Although some Zuni pursue traditional roles as farmers and herders and others are involved in the arts, most people earn their income from wages in a wide variety of occupations. According to statistics collected by the U.S. Census Bureau in 2000, 50.8 percent of the reservation population age 16 years or older were in the labor force. Of those, 41.1 percent were employed while 9.8 percent were unemployed. Statistics also illustrated that 49.2 percent were officially classified as "not in the labor force," meaning that they were no longer actively seeking work, possibly because they did not intend to work or because they were discouraged due to a lack of available jobs. The statistics on employment were roughly the same for men and women. These figures indicate a relative disadvantage for the Zuni when compared with other residents of New Mexico or the nation as a whole. In New Mexico in 2000, 60 percent of the population were employed; 4.8 percent were unemployed; and 35.2 percent were not in the labor force. In the same year, for the United States as a whole, 67.1 percent of the population were employed; 4.2 percent were unemployed; and 32.9 percent were not in the labor force.

Using somewhat different measures, data from 2007 indicate that 19.2 percent of Zuni age 25 or older were unemployed. Comparing these figures to those from 2000, rates of unemployment have just about doubled, indicating an economic downturn shared by most of the country.

Analyzed by "class of work," the largest category is that of government employment. That is, 43.8 percent of Zuni who are employed work for some government agency, either federal or local. In addition, 35.8 percent are privately employed while 20.2 percent are self-employed.

Within types of occupations reported in 2007, the largest percentage of Zuni workers are listed as working in educational services (17.4 percent), retail stores (13.9 percent), manufacturing (12.6 percent), public administration (11.3 percent), health care (9.7 percent), construction (9.1 percent), and social assistance (5.3 percent). Only 1.6 percent of the Zuni are engaged in agriculture, forestry, mining, and fishing and hunting. The gender distribution in these occupations is, as expected, somewhat uneven. A higher percentage of women than men work in education, health care, and social assistance, while more men work in public administration, construction, manufacturing, and farming, forestry, fishing, and mining. Men or women are as likely to work in retail sales, depending on the type of goods sold.

Consistent with the difficulty of finding jobs on or near their reservation, household and family incomes for the Zuni tend to be lower than for other residents of New Mexico or the nation.

On the Zuni Pueblo, the median household income was $27,876, while per-capita income was $8,813. In New Mexico, the median household income was $43,508, while per-capita income was $32,093. For the United States, the median household income was $50,233, while per-capita income was $39,392.

These data show that the Zuni household income is about half that of other U.S. residents, while the Zuni per-capita income is about one-fifth that of other Americans. The fact that the Zuni's per-capita income is much lower relative to the United States in general than their family income (one-fifth rather than one-half) reflects the larger size of Zuni families than is the American norm. Indeed, the median family size is 2.59 people for the United States and 2.6 for New Mexico, but the Zuni have a much higher average family size of 4.3 people. The Zuni pattern is consistent with that of Native Americans living on reservations.

Income is obviously related to statistics on poverty. As a consequence of their low incomes, the Zuni experience relatively greater levels of poverty than do other Americans: On the Zuni Pueblo, 43 percent of individuals live in poverty, compared with 18.4 percent of individuals in New Mexico and 23.7 percent of individuals in the United States.

The Zuni, therefore, are roughly twice as likely to live in poverty as are other residents of New Mexico and as other Americans. In fact, in 2008, 19.3 percent of Zuni residents had incomes below 50 percent of the poverty level, while the comparable figure for New Mexico was 7.8 percent. Finally, 36 percent of Zuni children lived in households with incomes below the poverty level, as compared with 25 percent of New Mexico's children.

Statistical information concerning educational attainment for the Zuni indicates a somewhat lower percentage of high school graduates than the national norm but a much lower percentage of college or university graduates. Among the Zuni, 63.7 percent are high school graduates while only 5.7 percent are college graduates. In New Mexico, 75.1 percent of the population are high school graduates while 20.4 percent are college graduates. And for the United States as a whole, 75.2 percent are high school graduates while 20.3 percent are college graduates.

Another 22.1 percent of Zuni have attended some college classes but have not received degrees, while 4.7 percent have their associate's degree and 1.9 percent hold graduate or professional degrees. Still, with lower rates of educational attainment, Zunis may lack some of the literacy and mathematical skills necessary for certain kinds of occupations, particularly higher-paying jobs. These data partially explain, or are at least consistent with, the data on employment and income.

Despite the lack of well-paying jobs in their own community, the population of the Zuni Reservation has continued to increase, its growth steady throughout the twentieth century. According to official U.S. Census Bureau figures for 2000, the number of people enrolled as members of the Zuni tribe stood at 10,122. Of these, 9,094 identified themselves as members of one tribe, while the remainder reported belonging to more than one Native group. The population of the Zuni Reservation, however, was 6,367 in 2000 but declined to 5,973 by 2007. Nearly all residents of the reservation are Zuni (97.4 percent). Most other residents are either Hispanic or white. These data together indicate that about two-thirds of the registered Zuni live on their reservation while about one-third live away from it. Rates of migration from reservations throughout the United States vary considerably. The patterns for the Zuni are within the norm and perhaps reflect a somewhat greater than average tendency to live on the reservation.

The Zuni population is fairly representative of the gender percentages in the country as a whole, having 3,100 females and 2,873 males (51.9 percent to 48.1 percent). The Zuni differ from general U.S. communities, however, in being a relatively young population. Their median age is 28.6 years, while the median age is 35 in the United States and 34.6 years in New Mexico. The youthful structure of the Zuni Reservation is a consequence of having relatively large families, at least as compared with other Americans.

An interesting insight into Zuni family organization is that in 48.9 percent of extended family households where grandparents are present and where there are children under 18, the grandparents are responsible as caregivers for their grandchildren. That is, grandparents are not merely additional residents of the households but are significant caretakers and as such are integral to the activities and functioning of the family.

Taken together, data on population trends and household composition indicate a strong sense of community and belonging. While there are economic difficulties due to the lack of jobs, people choose to remain on the reservation because of the sense of security and comfort afforded by living among a group with whom one develops a positive and nurturing identity.

A LIVING LANGUAGE

This identity is reflected, in part, in a vibrant tradition of maintaining the native Zuni language. According to U.S. Census Bureau data, an impressive 85.7 percent of Zuni speak their indigenous language at home, while 14.3 percent speak English only. Most of the Zuni speakers are bilinguals, able to converse in Zuni and English, but 29.2 percent report that they speak English "less than very well." Additional data on language indicate that the Zuni language is spoken by people in every age category, including a large number of young children. The census reports that 1,818 children ages 5 to 17 are fluent speakers of Zuni, thus ensuring continuation of the language into future generations, because it is the number of children speaking a language that reflects its vitality. These data contrast with trends for many other Native American languages still spoken in the United States, indicating that only a small number of languages have a significant group of young speakers, and therefore most Native languages will probably not be maintained much into the future.

To safeguard the Zuni language, elders attend and participate in Head Start programs at the elementary schools to encourage children to speak the language. Language immersion classes are held in higher grades as well. And the A:shiwi A:wan Museum and Heritage Center, as well as the local radio station, KSHI, conducts regularly scheduled programs in the Zuni language. As community member Edison Vicenti said in *Smithsonian* magazine, "If we lose our language, we lose the base of our religion and culture. And if we lose our religion, we lose what binds us together as Zuni. It is like the roots of a tree; if the tree is uprooted or the roots contaminated, then it dies. It is the same with us. And we can't let that happen."

In addition to their concerns about their land, economic development, and cultural rights, the Zuni are concerned about the health problems of their community. Doctors and researchers have focused on the very high levels of kidney disease and renal failure among Zuni. In particular, a study conducted in 1985 revealed that 1.6 percent of Zuni had renal disease, a figure that was 14 times the rate for U.S. whites and three times the rates for other Native Americans. Zuni of all ages, from young children to the elderly, are affected. About one-third of the cases of kidney disease were connected to diabetes, but the remainder were of unknown cause. A number of theories have been proposed, but none is certain. One theory suggests a genetic component, because there are strong family clusters of the disease and the Zuni community tends to be ethnically homogeneous. Another theory suggests some environmental causes or contributing factors, such as exposure to possibly toxic materials associated with making jewelry or pottery, or to some toxins in the water or salt consumed by the people.

Because of the seriousness of these ailments, the Zuni Tribal Council has agreed to cooperate with the Genetics Institute to study the prevalence of the disease among their people. By 2004, interviewers had spoken with nearly every member of the Zuni

In spite of all the obstacles that have threatened their existence, the Zuni have proved resilient and continue to preserve their culture both on and off the reservation. Above, two Zuni firefighters help contain a wildfire in New Mexico.

community. Researchers are collecting samples of DNA from many members to uncover any genetic factors that may predispose a person to develop kidney disease. They have also agreed to return all DNA samples to the Zuni community to establish a repository that will form the basis of future medical research on this and other ailments affecting the people.

As in all societies, differences of opinion exist among the Zuni about how best to strengthen their community, which paths to take for economic development, and how to merge tradition and change. These issues are discussed and debated at public meetings, as well as through conversations in a local paper formed in 1998, the *Shiwi Messenger,* which prints news articles and opinion pieces for the interchange of ideas.

The Zuni have demonstrated a remarkable ability to withstand centuries of intense pressure, first from Spanish invaders and even more from agents of U.S. control. Government officials, the military, missionaries, and teachers attempted to alter indigenous ways of life and systems of ethics. Of course, many Zuni activities have changed, as they have for all people. But a solid core of Zuni values and attitudes has remained strong, transmitted within families and in the community as a whole from generation to generation. In the words of James Enote, project leader of the Zuni Conservation Project and head of the Zuni Department of Natural Resources:

> For thousands of years we Zunis have lived in a complex and delicate environment which has sustained our ancestors and which continues to bring great benefits to our people today. But with the continuing growth of our population and the increasing demand for limited natural resources, the time has come to decide what means we will use to ensure that the resources and benefits available to our ancestors will be available for future generations.

Thinking about these issues is of paramount importance to the Zuni as they look to living in the twenty-first century. As Enote concludes, summing up the need to both conserve their land and resources and develop their economy:

> Today Zuni could probably be described as both a developing nation and a prosperous community. Our contemporary habits are approaching the patterns of the United States in general, but our culture and ways of life remain consistently and uniquely Zuni. We are faced with the enormous challenge of moving into the next century maintaining our traditions and values, yet needing the modern technical capability to deal with the conservation and development issues that confront us.

And finally, Zuni elders, as recorded in a Zuni publication, *The Zunis: Self-Portrayals,* offer reflections on the past and the future. As one elder said:

Many years ago when our grandparents foresaw what our future would be like, they spoke their prophecies among themselves and passed them on to the children before them. . . . But the people themselves will bring upon themselves what they receive. From what has resulted, time alone will tell what the future holds for us.

And another elder concluded:

Maybe it is because of the grandparents before our grandparents, who brought onto this land the ways of living and their thoughts of how their children should live, that the pattern in which we exist today is toil-less and peaceful. Should all our Zuni ways have been lost, our people today might not be as secure as they are. . . . We must just hope they, too, can survive what lies before them.

Chronology

A.D. 700–800   The Zuni's ancestors settle in their present-day territory, establishing several towns, most inhabited by about 100 people.

1300s   Six Zuni villages, including Hawikuh, a major center for intertribal trade in the Southwest, are established.

1539   The viceroy of the Spanish colony in Mexico sends Franciscan priest Marcos de Niza to explore the American Southwest. Although he never meets the Zuni, he claims

Timeline

A.D. 700–800

The Zuni's ancestors settle in their present-day territory

1540

Francisco Vásquez de Coronado's expedition arrives in Zuni territory; the Zuni battle the Spanish invaders to defend their villages

1863

President Abraham Lincoln presents a ceremonial cane to the Zuni governor, Mariano, as a sign of friendship

1600   **1875**

1300s

Six Zuni villages, including Hawikuh, a major center for intertribal trade in the Southwest, are established

1680

The Zuni join other Puebloan peoples in the Pueblo Revolt and move to a settlement on top of a mesa called Dowa Yalanne

1877

The Zuni Reservation is created by an executive order of President Rutherford B. Hayes

1917

An executive order by President Woodrow Wilson adds approximately 80,000 acres to the Zuni Reservation to have found wealthy cities, part of an empire he calls the Seven Cities of Cibola.

1540   Francisco Vásquez de Coronado's expedition arrives in Zuni territory; the Zuni battle the Spanish invaders to defend their villages; Coronado leaves Zuni territory and sets up headquarters of the new Spanish colony in the Pueblo village of Tiguex on the Rio Grande in New Mexico.

1632   Permanent Catholic missions in two Zuni villages are established, but the Zuni continue to resist Spanish colonial control.

1680   The Zuni join other Puebloan peoples in the Pueblo Revolt, killing their resident priest, burning church buildings, and expelling Spanish settlers who had intruded on their land. As a defensive measure, the Zuni abandon

1934

The stock-reduction program, instituted by the Bureau of Indian Affairs, divides the Zuni Reservation into 18 grazing units

1987

The U.S. Court of Indian Claims grants the Zuni title to a large portion of present-day Arizona and New Mexico

2003

In response to Zuni protests, the Salt River Project, a private utility company, abandons its plan to develop mining on land surrounding the sacred Zuni Salt Lake

2000   **2010**

1970

The Zuni adopt a formal constitution with a Zuni Tribal Council as their official legislative body

1990

Passage of the Zuni Land Conservation Act, which establishes a Zuni Indian Resource Development Trust Fund of $25 million to implement the Zuni Sustainable Resource Development Plan

2010

Zuni governor Norman Cooeyate testifies at a meeting sponsored by the United Nations to review the human rights record of member countries their villages and move to a settlement on top of a mesa called Dowa Yalanne, where they remain for 15 years.

1692   The Spanish reenter the Southwest from Mexico and regain control of most of the Puebloan towns along the Rio Grande. The Zuni, however, continue to resist complete Spanish control.

Late 1600s The Zuni begin to adopt some elements of the Spanish economy, particularly sheep and horses.

1705   The Zuni sign an agreement of friendship with the Spanish, allowing some Spanish presence in their territory in exchange for promises of protection from Apache and Navajo raiders.

1821   Mexican independence results in the shift in formal governance of Zuni territory from Spain to Mexico.

1848   The Treaty of Guadalupe Hidalgo is signed, ending the war between the United States and Mexico and transferring southwestern territory (the present-day states of New Mexico and Arizona) to the United States.

1863   President Abraham Lincoln presents a ceremonial cane to the Zuni governor, Mariano, as a sign of friendship.

1877   The Zuni Reservation is created by an executive order of President Rutherford B. Hayes; the reservation is only about one-tenth the size of Zuni territory before the European invasions.

1883   A second executive order is signed, adding some outlying areas to the reservation.

1897   The first government-run day school opens on the Zuni Reservation.

1917   An executive order by President Woodrow Wilson adds approximately 80,000 acres (32,374 hectares) to the Zuni Reservation. Additional parcels of land are added in 1935 and 1940, bringing the total to more than 400,000 acres (161,874 hectares).

1934   The stock-reduction program, instituted by the Bureau of Indian Affairs, divides the Zuni Reservation into

18 grazing units, each given a quota of livestock, and forces Zuni herders to reduce their stock of sheep.

1970   The Zuni adopt a formal constitution with a Zuni Tribal Council as their official legislative body.

1976   The Zuni Range Code, regulating livestock holdings, is created.

1977   The Zuni radio station KSHI-FM is founded.

1978   The Zuni obtain a lease to land surrounding Zuni Salt Lake, located 60 miles (97 kilometers) southwest of their reservation.

1984   The Zuni win the return of Koluwala-wa, a sacred land that was the site of pilgrimages for rain and good crops.

1987   The U.S. Court of Indian Claims grants the Zuni title to a large portion of present-day Arizona and New Mexico, stating that the tribe had been wrongfully deprived of nearly 15 million acres of land, and awards them $25 million as compensation.

1990   The federal Native American Graves Protection and Repatriation Act is passed after years of work by the Zuni to secure the return of some of their sacred objects; passage of the Zuni Land Conservation Act, which establishes a permanent Zuni Indian Resource Development Trust Fund of $25 million to implement the Zuni Sustainable Resource Development Plan; passage of the Indian Arts and Crafts Act intends to protect the authenticity of Native American jewelry and other craft products; formation of the Council for Indigenous Arts and Culture, based at the Zuni Reservation.

1995   The number of sacred objects successfully repatriated by the Zuni from various U.S. museums totals 80.

1998   The first Zuni newspaper, the *Shiwi Messenger,* is established.

2002   Zuni governor Malcolm Bowekaty testifies before the U.S. Senate Committee on Indian Affairs about the Zuni's desire to protect sacred objects and cultural resources; the

Zuni receive 75 pieces of pottery taken in the early twentieth century from Hawikuh.

2003 In response to Zuni protests, the Salt River Project, a private utility company, abandons its plan to develop mining on land surrounding the sacred Zuni Salt Lake.

2004 The U.S. Court of Appeals for the Ninth Circuit issues a ruling protecting sacred land at Woodruff Butte from mining and economic development; the Zuni sign an agreement with the Department of the Interior granting them 3,600 acre-feet (4.4 million cubic meters) of water to help restore water levels in "Zuni Heaven."

2010 Zuni governor Norman Cooeyate testifies at a meeting sponsored by the United Nations to review the human rights record of member countries. Cooeyate speaks about the efforts of Native tribes to persuade the U.S. government to recognize their rights to sacred sites.

Glossary

agent   A person appointed by the Bureau of Indian Affairs to supervise U.S. government programs on a reservation and/or in a specific region.

Awonawilona   The deity, who is both male and female, responsible for creating the universe.

Bow Priesthood   A prestigious group whose members were responsible for carrying out warfare and keeping order in the villages.

Bureau of Indian Affairs (BIA)   A federal government agency, now within the Department of the Interior, founded to manage relations with Native American tribes.

clan   A multigenerational group having a shared identity, organization, and property based on belief in their descent from a common ancestor. Because clan members consider themselves closely related, marriage within a clan is strictly prohibited.

culture   The learned behavior of humans; nonbiological, socially taught activities; the way of life of a group of people.

ethnologist   An anthropologist who specializes in comparing and analyzing different cultures.

fetish   A representative image of a deity made of wood and decorated with paint and feathers. Besides being a work of art, a fetish has great religious significance.

Indian Reorganization Act (IRA)   The 1934 federal law that ended the policy of allotting plots of land to individuals and encouraged the development of reservation communities. The act also provided for the creation of autonomous tribal governments.

itiwana   The middle place of the world, where the Zuni were told to settle after emerging from the inside of the earth in their creation legend.

kachinas   Souls of the dead who are impersonated by Zuni wearing special costumes and performing elaborate public dances. All Zuni men were members of one of the six kachina societies.

kiva A special square-shaped room, entered by a ladder through the ceiling, where religious ceremonies are held.

Koyemshis An ancient group of Raw People who are impersonated throughout the year. Also called the Mudheads, each Koyemshi acts like a clown but is considered to have great power to bring good fortune and rain.

lhamana A Zuni man who wore the clothing and performed the work traditionally associated with women. Tribal members considered lhamana (also known as berdaches) to be of a third gender, distinct from men and women.

matrilineal A kinship system based on descent from the woman's lineage.

Meriam Report A U.S. government study in 1928 that found appalling conditions of poverty on many reservations and suggested increased federal funding to Native American tribes.

metate A specialized grinding stone for making meal out of seeds, nuts, and corn.

Native American Graves Protection and Repatriation Act of 1990 A law that allows Native American tribes to repossess the artifacts and grave remains that were taken from them by museums and individual collectors.

Neweekwes Members of a Zuni medicine society who specialize in curing stomach ailments; the Neweekwes engage in sophisticated forms of clowning.

pekwin The head of Zuni village government who was appointed by the council of priests and worked with them to manage collective work, community affairs, and religious ceremonies. The pekwin was required to be a member of the Dogwood clan, as well as a kind and respected individual.

Rain Priesthood The most powerful priesthood, whose members derived their knowledge and powers from the Rain-Bringing Spirits and who performed rituals that would bring rain to the Zuni.

Raw People The many powerful deities and spirits in the Zuni religion, named for the raw food given to them as offerings from humans. The Zuni also say prayers and perform rituals in the Raw People's honor, and in exchange the Raw People provide protection and good fortune.

reservation   A tract of land retained by Indians for their own occupation and use.

Shalakos   Six powerful, birdlike beings who are impersonated by select Zuni men every fall and bring abundant crops and many children.

tribe   A society consisting of several separate communities united by kinship, culture, language, and other social institutions, including clans, religious organizations, and warrior societies.

Treaty of Guadalupe Hidalgo   The treaty that ended the U.S.-Mexican War in 1848 and granted the United States ownership of present-day Arizona and New Mexico. In the treaty, the U.S. government promised to respect the land and rights of the Native peoples in the region.

Zuni Land Conservation Act of 1990   As settlement of a Zuni lawsuit against the federal government, Congress established the Zuni Indian Resource Development Trust Fund of $25 million. Interest from the fund supports the Zuni Sustainable Resource Development Plan.

Zuni Tribal Council   Recognized by the U.S. government in the early 1970s, the Zuni's official legislative body has the right to control the local government and organize elections.

Bibliography

Books

Crampton, C. Gregory. *The Zunis of Cibola*. Salt Lake City: University of Utah Press, 1977.

Cushing, Frank Hamilton. *Cushing at Zuni: The Correspondence and Journals of Frank Hamilton Cushing, 1879–1884*, edited by Jesse Green. Albuquerque: University of New Mexico Press, 1990.

———. *Zuni Folk Tales*. 1901. Reprint. Tucson: University of Arizona Press, 1986.

———. *Zuni: Selected Writings of Frank Hamilton Cushing*, edited by Jesse Green. Lincoln: University of Nebraska Press, 1979.

Dozier, Edward. *The Pueblo Indians of North America*. New York: Holt, Rinehart & Winston, 1970.

Ferguson, T.J., and E.R. Hart. *A Zuni Atlas*. Norman: University of Oklahoma Press, 1985.

Hart, E. Richard, ed. *Zuni and the Courts: A Struggle for Sovereign Land Rights*. Lawrence: University Press of Kansas, 1995.

Morris, John Miller. *From Coronado to Escalante: The Explorers of the Spanish Southwest*. New York: Chelsea House, 1992.

Ortiz, Alfonso, ed. *Handbook of North American Indians: Southwest*. Vol. 9. Washington, D.C.: Smithsonian Institution Press, 1979.

———. *The Pueblo*. New York: Chelsea House, 1994.

Ostler, James, Marian Rodee, and Milford Nahohai. *Zuni: A Village of Silversmiths*. Zuni, N.M.: A:Shiwi Publishers, 1996.

Pollock, Penny. *The Turkey Girl: A Zuni Cinderella Story*. Boston, Mass.: Little, Brown, and Company, 1996.

Rosier, Paul. *Serving Their Country: American Indian Politics and Patriotism in the Twentieth Century*. Cambridge, Mass.: Harvard University Press.

Tedlock, Barbara. *The Beautiful and the Dangerous: Encounters with the Zuni Indians*. New York: Viking, 1992.

Wilson, Edmund. *Red, Black, Blond and Olive: Studies in Four Civilizations: Zuni, Haiti, Soviet Russia, Israel*. New York: Oxford University Press, 1956.

Wright, Barton. *Kachinas of the Zuni.* Flagstaff, Ariz.: Northland Press, 1985.

Wyaco, Virgil. *A Zuni Life: A Pueblo Indian in Two Worlds.* Albuquerque: University of New Mexico Press, 1998.

The Zuni People. *Zunis: Self-portrayals.* Translated by Alvina Quam. Albuquerque: University of New Mexico Press, 1972.

Articles

Baxter, Paula. "Cross-cultural Controversies in the Design History of Southwestern American Indian Jewellery." *Journal of Design History,* vol. 7, no. 4 (1994): 233–245.

Ferguson, T.J., Roger Anyon, and Edmund Ladd. "Repatriation at the Pueblo of Zuni: Diverse Solutions to Complex Problems." *American Indian Quarterly,* vol. 20, no. 2 (Spring 1996): 251–273.

Howell, Todd. "Tracking Zuni Gender and Leadership Roles Across the Contact Period." *Journal of Anthropological Research,* vol. 51, no. 2 (Summer 1995): 125–147.

Kintigh, Keith, Donna M. Glowacki, and Deborah L. Huntley. "Long-term Settlement History and the Emergence of Towns in the Zuni Area." *American Antiquity,* vol. 69, no. 3 (July 2004): 432–456.

McMillen, Christian. "Rain, Ritual, and Reclamation: The Failure of Irrigation on the Zuni and Navajo Reservations, 1883–1914." *Western Historical Quarterly,* vol. 31, no. 4 (Winter 2000): 435–456.

Mills, Barbara J. "Gender and the Reorganization of Historic Zuni Craft Production: Implications for Archaeological Interpretation." *Journal of Anthropological Research,* vol. 51, no. 2 (Summer 1995): 149–172.

Morell, Virginia. "The Zuni Way." *Smithsonian,* April 2007: 76–83.

Walker, Willard. "Palowahtiwa and the Economic Redevelopment of Zuni Pueblo." *Ethnohistory,* vol. 21, no. 1 (Winter 1974): 65–75.

Watts, Linda. "Zuni Family Ties and Household-group Values: A Revisionist Cultural Model of Zuni Social Organization." *Journal of Anthropological Research,* vol. 53, no. 1 (Spring 1997): 17–29.

Wessel, Thomas R. "Phantom Experiment Station: Government Agriculture on the Zuni Reservation." *Agricultural History,* vol. 61, no. 4 (Autumn 1987): 1–12.

Selections from *Handbook of North American Indians: Southwest.* Vol. 9. Alfonso Ortiz, ed. Washington, D.C.: Smithsonian Institution Press, 1979.

Eggan, Fred. "Pueblos: Introduction."

Eggan, Fred, and T.N. Pandey. "Zuni History, 1850–1970."

Ladd, Edmund. "Zuni Economy."
———. "Zuni Social and Political Organization."
Sando, Joe. "The Pueblo Revolt."
Simmons, Marc. "History of Pueblo-Spanish Relations to 1821."
———. "History of the Pueblos Since 1821."
Tedlock, Dennis. "Zuni Religion and World View."
Woodbury, Richard. "Zuni Prehistory and History to 1850."

Web Sites

A:shiwi A:wan Museum and Heritage Center
http://www.ashiwi-museum.org/

A:shiwi News, **Zuni Newspaper**
http://www.ashiwi.org/AshiwiNews.aspx

Information on the Zuni
http://www.crystalinks.com/zuni.html

Pueblo of Zuni
http://www.ashiwi.org

Zuni Origin Myths
http://www.sacred-texts.com/nam/zuni/bunzel/zom.htm

Further Resources

Kessell, John L. *Pueblos, Spaniards, and the Kingdom of New Mexico.* Norman: University of Oklahoma Press, 2010.

McManis, Kent. *Zuni Fetishes and Carvings.* Tucson, Ariz.: Rio Nuevo Press, 2010.

Web Sites

Experience Zuni Pueblo
http://www.zunitourism.com/

Indian Pueblo Cultural Center
http://www.indianpueblo.org/

Zuni Indian Language
http://www.native-languages.org/zuni.htm

Zuni Spirits: Fine Zuni Fetish Carvings
http://www.zunispirits.com/

Picture Credits

Index

About the Contributors

NANCY BONVILLAIN received her Ph.D. in anthropology and linguistics from Columbia University. Her major fields of research and writing include Native American culture and history and Iroquoian linguistics. She has prepared teaching materials for the Mohawk language, in addition to writing four textbooks. Dr. Bonvillain has written several books on Native American societies and leaders for Chelsea House.

Series editor **PAUL C. ROSIER** received his Ph.D. in American history from the University of Rochester in 1998. Dr. Rosier currently serves as associate professor of history at Villanova University (Villanova, Pennsylvania), where he teaches Native American History, American Environmental History, Global Environmental Justice Movements, History of American Capitalism, and World History.

In 2001, the University of Nebraska Press published his first book, *Rebirth of the Blackfeet Nation, 1912–1954;* in 2003, Greenwood Press published *Native American Issues* as part of its Contemporary Ethnic American Issues series. In 2006, he coedited an international volume called *Echoes from the Poisoned Well: Global Memories of Environmental Injustice.* Dr. Rosier has also published articles in the *American Indian Culture and Research Journal,* the *Journal of American Ethnic History,* and the *Journal of American History.* His *Journal of American History* article, titled "They Are Ancestral Homelands: Race, Place, and Politics in Cold War Native America, 1945–1961," was selected for inclusion in *The Ten Best History Essays of 2006–2007,* published by Palgrave MacMillan in 2008; and it won the Western History Association's 2007 Arrell Gibson Award for Best Essay on the history of Native Americans. His latest book, *Serving Their Country: American Indian Politics and Patriotism in the Twentieth Century* (Harvard University Press), is winner of the 2010 Labriola Center American Indian National Book Award.